WORDS WE USE

WORDS WE USE

A Glossary and Reference
Guide for Publishing and Media

MS IN PUBLISHING PROGRAM
PACE UNIVERSITY

Published by Pace University Press
41 Park Row
New York, NY 10038

PUPText, an imprint of Pace University Press

ISBN 978-1-935625-88-9

Cover Design by Ariel Stevenson and Sara Yager

CIP data available

Printed in the United States of America

24 25 26 27 28   1 3 5 7 9 10 8 6 4 2
First Edition

Kirsten Sandberg
Editor-in-Chief, Blockchain Research Institute
Adjunct Faculty

Manuela Soares
Director, MS in Publishing
Director, Pace University Press

Jason Wells
Marketing Director, APA Style, APA Books,
LifeTools Nonfiction, and Magination Press Children's Books,
The American Psychological Association
Adjunct Faculty

Veronica Wilson
National Digital Sales Director, Dotdash Meredith
Adjunct Faculty

CONTENTS

ACKNOWLEDGMENTS

This book would not have been possible without the generous contributions of our Editorial Board and students, alums, and friends of the program, especially: Harshdeep Kaur (Student Aide), Kayleigh Woltal (Graduate Assistant), Erin Hurley (Graduate Assistant), Kaitlyn Keel (Graduate Assistant), Shianne Henion (Graduate Assistant), Ariel Stevenson (Graduate Assistant), Harper Bullard (Student Aide), Liz Abrams (Student Aide), Lucely Garcia (Production Associate), and Clare Perret (alum). A very special thank you to Sara Yager, who has assisted the Press with her design expertise on past projects and on this book.

EDITORIAL NOTE

In Pace University's MS in Publishing program, students learn every aspect of the publishing chain from content creation and acquisition to the final designed product and every step in between: editorial, marketing, sales, and more. In doing so, students learn the language of books and magazines, print and digital media production.

Every industry has its own particular vocabulary, words used to communicate internally and externally. Language and communication skills are a part of any publishing program's curriculum. Using and understanding the language appropriate to a specific department or task is necessary for success in the publishing industry.

It often surprises and delights me to discover a new word in my everyday life. Professionally, it is important to understand the language of any discipline in order to communicate effectively. Though there are many lists available on the web, I have not seen a comprehensive reference guide to the core words used in the publishing industry. Even publishing veterans are sometimes surprised by a new word or learning what an acronym means for a word they have used for years.

This glossary provides an overview of the terms publishing professionals use in every department, from editorial to sales. In some cases the language is similar in books and magazines, digital media or comics, but may have a different meaning. This guide includes those differences.

The words used in publishing and media are a distinct and essential part of our ability to communicate with each other. Language is not static and the language in publishing has grown, changed, and continues to evolve in our digital world. The industry has progressed digitally and some of the language that has developed along with that growth is included here. You will find words new and old, common usage and more esoteric terms reflecting new digital realities.

This glossary also addresses our changing industry and provides some related information specific to publishing—the elements of a

Media Kit, a list of publishing and related organizations, the reference guides used in publishing and media, and additional glossaries that address other areas of publishing, from educational terms to words used in Artificial Intelligence.

In publishing and media, we often learn only those words relevant to our specific jobs or departments, and not to other departments or to publishing as a whole. In this glossary of terms, you will find a comprehensive list of words that are used throughout publishing and media. Knowing this publishing vocabulary enhances our ability to communicate with each other and to better understand every aspect of the publishing industry.

We created this glossary first for our students and faculty, but also for the industry as a whole. We hope they find *Words We Use* to be informative and useful.

Manuela Soares, Director
MS in Publishing Program
Pace University Press

GLOSSARY

A

A/B testing
The process of comparing two variations of a single variable to determine which performs best in order to help improve marketing efforts. This is often done in email marketing (with variations in the subject line or copy), calls to action (variations in colors or verbiage), landing pages (variations in content), and in digital ads (variations in messaging or image).

accessibility
Formats that are accessible to visually impaired persons, in particular audio books and electronic formats. See **web accessibility**

acknowledgments
Though it can be part of the front matter or back matter, acknowledgments are often in the front matter. In this section, an author or editor can acknowledge and thank people who may have been helpful during the writing or publishing process.

acquisition
The process of finding and acquiring manuscripts for publication. The acquisition process often starts with a literary agent pitching a book to an editor and ends with either the acquisition by the editor or a rejection.

acquisition editor (also known as an acquiring editor)
The editor who works with authors and agents to acquire manuscripts for publication, presenting a potential book project to their publisher, editorial director, or editorial board.

acquisition meeting
The meeting where a company's editors present the titles they are hoping to acquire to their editorial board, usually composed of senior level editorial, marketing, and sales staff. These prospective titles are either approved, rejected, or returned for additional information.

advance
Money given to an author by a publisher before a book is published. This "advance" of monies is almost always against (i.e., subtracted from) future royalties. Often paid in increments, for example, half of the advance on signing the contract, half on delivery and acceptance of the full manuscript.

Advanced Ship Notice (ASN)
Barcodes on delivery cartons containing vendor provided details on the contents of each carton.

Advanced Reader's Copies (ARC)
Also known as Advanced Reader's Editions, ARCs are a marketing tool used prior to publication. ARCs look like a trade paperback and are created for hardcover fiction or nonfiction (not illustrated) top tier titles to send to reviewers, bookstore buyers, and others. Unlike bound galleys (which are xeroxed in quantities of 300–500), ARCs are printed in quantities of 1500 or more and usually have marketing copy on the cover.

advertisers
Businesses that purchase advertising space for their company and their products in any media.

advertising
A paid public communication for a company or product designed to attract viewers, pique interest, and encourage them to take action.

advertising agencies
Businesses that develop and prepare advertising plans, ads, and other promotional tools for advertisers. Ad agencies also purchase space and reserve time in a variety of media.

advertising campaign
A group of ads with a specific message and goal. Ad campaigns can be used to create brand awareness and drive sales.

advertising conversion
Ad conversion occurs when a consumer takes action as a result of an ad. The action can be making a purchase, signing up for a newsletter, or filling out a web form. Any action that the user might take after being exposed to an ad.

advertising exchange
An ad exchange is a digital marketplace that connects supply side platforms (SSP) with demand side platforms (DSP) so that they can buy and sell ad space in real-time.

advertising impression
Also referred to as an "ad view," impressions are used primarily in online advertising, and represent the digital views for an ad, digital post, or web page. This doesn't represent "clicks," but the number of times the ad has been viewed.

advertising media
The different mass media or alternative media channels where a company can promote their products, services, or brand.

advertising technology
AdTech is the term that describes the digital tools and technologies used to reach audiences and measure digital advertising campaigns. AdTech includes a variety of tools and technologies that help advertisers provide relevant ads to the right audience.

afterword
Part of the back matter, an afterword can be written by the author or someone else and concludes the book. It often focuses on the topic of the book or the process of writing it.

agate
An extremely small size of type that is a little over thirteen lines in an inch. Used primarily for ads in magazines; an agate is half the size of a pica.

agent (or literary agent)
A literary agent reviews manuscripts and selects authors to represent and then pitches those manuscripts to a publisher or editor. Agents submit an author's work and negotiate contracts with the publisher and others. Agents work on commission, charging 15% or more for their services.

aggregators
A company that acts as an intermediary between authors and distributors and are used by self-published authors.

appendix
Part of the back matter, an appendix (or appendices) provides supplementary information related to the subject of the book.

Application Prgramming Interfaces (API)
A standard set of protocols that enables communication between applications and also allows them to exchange information.

art director (AD)
The person responsible for the overall design of a book, the AD works with designers and artists to create a cover and interior design. In some instances in book publishing, the art director works on both the cover and interiors, and in others, the AD who creates the cover design is not the same as the AD who designs the interiors.

Artificial Intelligence (AI)
A simulation of human intelligence by a computer system. With AI, a computer can think and learn and is able to complete tasks that are usually done by people, such as language processing,

problem-solving, learning, and exercising creativity.

ascender
The part of a lowercase letter, such as the stem of a lowercase b or d that extends above the x-height and usually above the cap height.

Atom feed
An Atom feed is similar to an RSS feed used to distribute web content, such as blog posts, news articles, and podcasts, in a standardized way. Atom was developed as a modern and more flexible alternative to RSS and is based on XML and namespaces to make the formatting easier to extend and maintain over time. See **Really Simple Syndication (RSS), Extensible Markup Language (XML)**

auction
One of the methods agents use to sell a book to an editor. Book auctions involve more than one publisher bidding on a project. Usually the publisher who makes the best offer (including advance, royalties, rights) will win. There are several ways to run an auction, including a pre-empt, when a publisher offers a high enough amount to persuade an agent to cancel the auction and accept the high bid.

audience
The person or people, based on quantifiable factors such as age, ethnicity, income, occupation, and other factors, who might be interested in a company or product.

audiobook
A book that is read aloud and available on a variety of media – cassette, CD, digital download, or streaming.

Audit Bureau of Circulations (ABI)
A not-for-profit, voluntary organization made up of magazine publishers, advertisers, and advertising agencies that audits and verifies a magazine publisher's circulation figures.

author's alteration (AA)
Used when marking a correction made to layouts or proofs by the author.

authority file
Extended list of records including "see also" references. New entries are matched to the authority in order to obtain standardized and consistent output. Typically used for subjects, contributors, publisher names, and titles when creating bibliographic data.

B

back matter
Supplementary pages at the end of a book that provide additional information. Back matter can include an afterword, appendix, author bio, author note, back of book ad, bibliography, colophon, contributor list or bios, epilogue, glossary, index, artwork, and photography credits, suggested reading. See **Appendix D: Front and Back Matter**

Back of Book
In advertising, the section of a magazine (or book) that follows the main body of editorial matter.

Back of Book Ad (BOB)
A display ad in the back matter of a book that showcases other books either by the same author, another book in the series, or backlist books by another author.

backlist
Backlist are those titles that have been previously published, typically in the past year or two.

balloon
In comics: the balloon is the basic unit of dialogue (Speech Balloon) or thought (Thought Balloon) as expressed by a

character in a panel. Variations include different outlining to indicate a whisper, a shout, or electronic communication, for example.

banner ad

The first type of internet-specific advertising, created in 1994, a banner ad is a rectangular graphic display on a web site or online platform that extends across the top, bottom, or sides of the page.

bar code

A pattern of parallel lines of varying widths, printed on, and identifying a product in a visual, machine-readable form. They play a key role in supply chains, enabling retailers and manufacturers to track information about the product, such as ISBN and retail price.

baseline

This is the imaginary line upon which letters rest. It's used as a point from which other elements are measured.

belly band

In Magazine publishing: A promotional paper band wrapped around the magazine after it is printed and bound.

In Book publishing: A promotional paper band wrapped around the book on top of the jacket after the book is printed and bound. Sometimes belly bands are used with a paper over board cover. Generally they are only a few inches high.

Bibliographic Framework Initiative (BIBFRAME)

Initiated by the Library of Congress, BIBFRAME provides a foundation for the future of bibliographic description, both on the web and in the broader networked world that is grounded in Linked Data techniques. A major focus of the initiative is to determine a transition path for the MARC 21 formats while preserving a robust data exchange that has supported resource sharing and cataloging cost savings in recent decades.

bibliography

A part of the back matter, a bibliography is a list of the written works (books, magazines, journals, and other source material) that were used to research and write the book that includes all of the publication details including title, author, publisher, and date of publication.

bind-in card

Most magazines include inserted or blown in subscription promotion cards. See **blow-in**

binder boards

The three pieces of stiff cardboard used to create the case for a hardcover book: front cover, back cover, and the spine.

binding

How the pages of a print book are secured, i.e., either sewn or glued or stapled between cover materials.

bio

A brief description of an author or a writer used on a book jacket or on promotional and marketing materials.

BLAD

This term is an acronym for Basic (or Book) Layout and Design and used for illustrated books. A BLAD is a 4 to 16 page brochure, usually produced in four-color, and used as a sales and marketing/publicity tool. A BLAD is usually created for big illustrated books to show the major elements of the book. See **Machine Readable Cataloging (MARC)**

bleed

A printing term, it refers to the printed area that extends past where the publication will be trimmed, generally images, background colors, or graphics. The bleed is an extra 1/8 of an inch past the trim, so it appears to be bleeding off the page.

blow-in card

A subscription promotion card or envelope blown loosely into a magazine so that it will fall out and attract attention.

blues (or bluelines)

A blue-print copy from the printer of the entire book made from film. Generally the last step before printing plates are created, and the last opportunity to make any changes before a book is printed. In the digital age, bluelines are rarely used, proofs are printed and look like the finished book in paperback format.

Many publishers see digital proofs of book interiors from the printers to replace this blues stage—yet still call them blues.

blurb

A short promotional description or a book endorsement by a well-known or expert name sometimes used for a front or back cover or as a list with other blurbs in the front matter. Blurbs can also be added to company websites and e-retailers such as Amazon, BN.com, BookShop.org, and others.

board book

A book for very young children, generally square in format and printed on heavy cardboard with both the cover and the interior pages printed on the same cardboard stock.

body copy

The main part of the text of a book that appears between the front and back matter. Also used in advertising and refers to the main text of the ad.

boilerplate

Standard clauses in a contract. Most clauses in a contract may be negotiated, but other clauses may not be changed, i.e., boilerplate. This term can also describe a block of copy that is used in marketing/publicity materials which supply basic information about the publishing house.

book

A written and printed work where the pages are glued or sewn together and bound between covers. Usually at least 64 pages in length.

book block

Folded signatures that are not yet bound with the cover, but stacked in sequence and sewn or glued together prior to binding with the cover. See **smyth sewn, signature**

Book Industry Communication (BIC)

A British organization that promotes increased efficiency in the supply chain for book and magazine industries (physical and electronic) by the development and use of standard processes and procedures. Sponsored and funded in part by several groups: the Publishers' Association, Booksellers' Association, the Chartered Institute of Library and Information Professionals, and the British Library.

A minimal set of metadata elements needed for a book as prescribed by the UK book industry.

Book Industry Standards and Communication Codes (BISAC)

BISAC codes are a way to categorize books. These nine-character alphanumeric codes (three letters followed by 6 digits) are assigned to every book and help book retailers, distributors, and librarians to assign their own categories and subcategories for a book.

Book Industry Study Group (BISG)

A US membership organization made up of publishers, manufacturers, wholesalers and distributors, libraries, retailers, and industry partners. Their focus is solving problems that affect two or more parts of the industry in five core areas: metadata, rights, supply chain, subject codes (BISAC), and workflow. See **Book Industry Standards and Communication Codes**

book launch

Any event or activity to promote the release of a new title.

book proposal

A book proposal is created by an author and/or literary agent to submit to a potential publisher to consider for acquisition. It includes a synopsis of the book, sample chapters, and a marketing plan. When submitting a proposal for a nonfiction work, an outline and brief description of each chapter is necessary. For a work of fiction, sample chapters are enough for the proposal, but the full manuscript should also be available. Nonfiction is often acquired with a proposal, but with fiction, once interest has been established, a publisher will want to see the entire manuscript before making an offer.

book signing

An event at a bookstore or other venue that is publicized and features the author reading from their book, answering questions from attendees, and autographing books.

bookstore chains

Chain bookstores refer to organizations that have more than one or two brick and mortar locations and primarily sell books. Bookstore chains include national chains such as Barnes & Noble, Books-A-Million, and Follett's, and regional chains such as Bookman's, Powell's, and Tattered Cover.

border

A border is a printed line, decorative line, shadow, or box around text or art on a printed page.

bound galley

Galleys are taken from composed type (i.e., all type design specifications including correct margin width, leading, typefaces, and type sizes), before final page composition. In the past, galleys were typically xeroxed pages bound with a four-color cover and distributed in smaller numbers (under 500-1000), unlike an ARC, which is printed in larger quantities. E-galleys have taken the place of print galleys, though ARCs are still done for books that are expected to sell well. See **Advanced Reader's Copy**

burst binding

This type of binding is created by first having the signatures perforated in the crease of the fold on press or when folded. This perforation allows the glue to sink in further. See **glued binding**, **notch binding**, and **smyth-sewn**

Business-to-Business (B2B)

A B2B business sells products or services to other businesses. In digital publishing, these businesses are often seen as thought leaders in their niche spaces.

Business-to-Consumer (B2C)

A B2C business deals directly with consumers, like a bookstore or a café. In digital publishing, B2C companies often focus on creating a community around their brand and providing good customer service.

byline

The name of the writer of a magazine or journal article or essay.

C

Call to Action (CTA)

A directive, image, or button intended to persuade a reader to perform a specific act on a web site, landing page, or app. (Ex: "buy now," "click here," or "learn more")

cap height
The height of the uppercase letters in a typeface. Often a bit lower than the ascender height; cap height can vary between typefaces.

caption
A short descriptive explanation for an illustration, graphic, or photo. In comics, the usually rectangular copy blocks that are used for narrative voice.

card page
Part of the front matter, a card page is a list of the other works by the same author or publisher.

Cascading Style Sheet (CSS)
CSS is a stylesheet language that describes the look and format of a document written in HTML or XML and how they will appear on screen, on paper, or on other media.

case binding
Also called a hardcover binding. Case binding refers to the case that protects the text or book block, usually made of cardboard with a printed cover or other material glued to it. The book block is glued or sewn into the case.

casewrap
A hardcover book where the case is wrapped in a printed sheet of paper, similar to paper-over-board. Often used for cookbooks, poetry books, textbooks, manuals, and reference books.

castoff
Usually done by the art department, the castoff is an estimate of the number of pages a manuscript will take up when typeset (for example, 120 manuscript pages might create an 80-page typeset book, depending on the design of the page, i.e., font, leading, margins).

Cataloging in Publication (CIP)
Created by the Library of Congress, CIP data is a bibliographic record that appears printed on the copyright page.

It is an abbreviated version of the machine-readable cataloging (or MARC) record in the Library's database which is distributed to libraries and book vendors.

chapbook
A shorter length book, usually about 40 pages. They can be perfect bound or bound with a saddle stitch. Historically, chapbooks were inexpensive books that were sold to working class readers. In today's world, chapbooks are often books of poetry, but they have been used as marketing tools by several publishers who published excerpts from full-length works as a chapbook as part of their marketing efforts.

chapter books
In children's publishing, a story that is aimed at intermediate readers, generally readers aged 7 to 10. Unlike a picture book, chapter books are primarily told through prose not pictures.

character count
The number of letters that are present in a piece of text.

ChatGPT (Chat Generative Pre-trained Transformer)
A language processing tool developed by OpenAI that uses artificial intelligence to generate text.

CHORUS (Clearing house for the Open Research of the United States)
A database that facilitates identification, discovery, and preservation of Open Access works. Funders, societies, publishers, institutions, and the public are able to view content, analysis, and metadata. See **Open Access**

circulation
Generally used by the magazine industry, circulation indicates the number of copies distributed for a given magazine title. A subset of this are audience

figures for TV shows, listenership for radio/podcasts, and UVPM/Hits for websites. It is a metric that indicates the outlet's reach, and can differ by paid subscription v. pass along rate (ex: a doctor's office may hold a subscription for a publication, but potentially X number of patients can read the same issue in the waiting room).

CMYK (Cyan Magenta Yellow Black)
CMYK refers to the preferred color system for any printed matter. It layers four ink plates—cyan, magenta, yellow, and black (which is also called the key color because it holds the detail in the image), to create printed images of any color. See **RGB**

co-edition
An edition of a book published simultaneously by publishers in different countries in different languages, often used for illustrated books. The printing is managed by the originating publisher who creates each edition through a black plate change—changing the language of the text, but leaving all of the four-color page layouts the same in each edition. This is different from foreign rights. See **foreign rights**

colophon
The colophon is a note, usually on the last page of a book that describes the individuals, companies, materials, and processes involved in producing the book. Colophon can also refer to a publisher's logo, typically placed on the spine or title page of a book.

color palette
A color palette is a combination of colors used in graphic design. There are four main color palettes:

1. Monochromatic: different shades of the same color.

2. Analogous: using a small number of adjacent colors on a color wheel. Pick a

color and use that and the color to the left and right of it.

3. Complementary: a color scheme that uses one color on the color wheel and another color from the opposite side of the wheel. This generally produces high-contrast combinations of colors.

4. Triadic: three colors evenly spaced around a color wheel. If there are 12 colors on the wheel, starting anywhere on the wheel, a triadic color palette would use colors equidistant from each other.

color wheel
Originally created by Sir Isaac Newton, a color wheel is a circular diagram and arrangement of colors organized by their chromatic relationship to each other. The primary colors are equidistant from each other on the wheel, and secondary and tertiary colors are between them. A useful aid for artists and designers.

coloring
In comics, the skill exercised by a colorist to add tonal qualities to artwork created in black and white.

colorist
A term used in comics for the person who adds color to the final art.

comp titles
Comp is short for comparable. Comp titles are books that might appeal to the same readers as the book an editor is trying to acquire. These titles are used by the acquisitions team before signing a book as a metric to gauge audience interest and sales potential. Comp titles may also be used during the creation of publicity and marketing plans.

composition order
Instructions to the typesetter from Design/Production. These include the project specs and details about the text elements, including margins, font,

chapter or section openers, running heads, and folios.

compositor (or typesetter)
Flows the text into the interior design, being careful to avoid awkward breaks that impede legibility.

concept book
A term used in children's book publishing, it refers to an illustrated book (picture book or board book) aimed at pre-school age children that teaches a basic concept such as the alphabet, shapes, sizes, numbers, or colors. These types of books typically have very few words. See **high concept**

content
Written, visual, audio, or other types of informational material meant to be shared with the public.

Content Management System (CMS)
A web application designed to make it easy for non-technical users to create, edit, and manage a website (Example: Wordpress)

cookies
Data that is stored on your computer when you access a web site. These small files often include unique identifiers that allow a website to remember a visitor, their preferences, and online habits.

co-op monies
This refers to cooperative advertising and is a way for book publishers to share the costs of advertising and promotion for their titles with the bookstores who carry them. It is usually calculated on a percentage basis of previous year's sales of books by that publisher with the bookstore.

copyediting
An editorial function that focuses on making the text clear, correct, concise, comprehensible, and consistent.

Copyediting focuses on text sentence by sentence, checking for accuracy, consistency, and errors in grammar, spelling, syntax, and punctuation.

copyright
According to the US Copyright Office, copyright is a type of intellectual property that protects original works of authorship as soon as an author fixes the work in a tangible form of expression. A copyright is the exclusive right to reproduce the work, create derivatives of the work, distribute copies of the work for free or through sales or rentals, display and perform the work publicly in physical and digital formats and media, and license or transfer any of these rights to another party. Copyright law covers many different types of original works, including paintings, photographs, illustrations, musical compositions, sound recordings, computer programs, books, poems, blog posts, movies, architectural works, plays, and more.

copywriting
Mainly used in advertising, the goal of copywriting is to convince a consumer to try a product.

Cost Per Thousand (CPM)
A marketing term describing the cost of reaching 1,000 people in a specific medium's audience. The CPM can help measure the effectiveness of advertising and determines how much an advertiser pays per click.

Creative Commons
A non-profit international organization that helps overcome legal obstacles to the sharing of knowledge and creativity. The organization provides Creative Commons licenses and public domain tools that they say gives both people and organizations a "free, simple, and standardized way to grant copyright permissions for creative and academic works; ensure proper attribution; and

allow others to copy, distribute, and make use of those works."

crop

Cutting out parts of an image from the side, top, or bottom to allow for a different emphasis.

crowdfunding

The process of marketing and funding publications through websites such as Kickstarter, Zoop, Indiegogo, and others, where consumers pledge funds prior to actually being given the product.

D

DAISY

This is the acronym for Digital Accessible Information System, a format for digital talking books for people who have a print disability or are blind.

DAISY Consortium

An organization that creates web accessibility standards (including ebook accessibility standards) and tools for testing accessibility.

data ecosystem

A data ecosystem refers to the general infrastructure of an organization and the methods it uses to collect, store, analyze, and leverage data, including programming languages, packages, algorithms, and cloud-computing services. Also referred to as a technology stack, a data ecosystem allows organizations to have a better understanding of their customers in order to improve their marketing, pricing, and operations strategies.

debossing

Embossing and debossing are the two main forms of stamping that can be used on a jacket. Debossing means the image or lettering is pressed into the jacket, below its surface. Debossing can also be used on a hardcover case.

dedication

Often given its own page in a book in the front matter, where the author thanks or acknowledges a specific person or group.

Demand Side Platform (DSP)

Software that automates the process of an advertiser buying ad space.

descender

The downward vertical stroke such as the stem of a lowercase letter in a g or p that extends below the baseline.

design memo (also called a planning memo)

Describes the organization of the book including the specs and structure and the elements that will be present in the book (such as illustrations and index) and where they are likely to be located. The design memo also lays out preliminary pagination.

developmental edit

Developmental editing focuses on the overall book in terms of character, plot, clarity, and structure and occurs before a manuscript goes to production for copy editing. The editor works with the author during this process to suggest and make these types of broad changes.

Dewey Decimal System

Shelf location system used by public and school libraries. Each book is assigned a number on their spine label and books are shelved in order of these numbers.

die stamp

A steel die cut to a specific shape and then used to stamp or impress that shape onto a surface, such as a cloth book cover. Die-stamping can be a synonym for foil-stamping, though ink is often used instead of foil. If a die-stamp is used without any foil or ink, it is called blind-stamping.

Digital Object Identifier (DOI)
Identifies an intellectual property of any type. Can be any level of granularity. Also serves as a persistent URL for that object.

Digital Rights Management (DRM)
Technology, i.e., software, that publishers use to control and protect their copyrighted creative materials: text, images, contracts, video, audio.

dingbat
In typography, a dingbat is a decorative element or character often used to mark divisions between sections of text or to indicate missing letters.

direct buys
In publishing, this occurs when a media buyer negotiates ad rates and run times on a web site or traditional publication directly with a publisher.

direct mail
A method of promoting books by mailing printed material such as a postcard or flyer directly to potential buyers.

display ad
An ad in a print publication, web site, or app that uses graphics and text and is created to attract attention for a product or service and can be interactive or include a Call to Action.

distributor
Companies that work with publishers to distribute their books to bookstores and other retailers. A publisher might sign a unique agreement per geographic market with a distributor who will ship/invoice books for them. The distributor may also handle marketing and sales for the publisher. Major distributors include Ingram and Baker & Taylor and specialized distributors such as Distributed Art Publishers (DAP), which represents publishers focused primarily on art, design, and photography. Large publishers such as Penguin Random House and Macmillan also handle distribution for smaller publishers.

Dots Per Inch (DPI)
DPI is used to describe the resolution of an image on monitors, printers, and scanners, typically 72, 300, and 1200 respectively. (A minimum of 300 dpi is required for print.) See **resolution**

draft
An unfinished manuscript or piece of writing that has not been published.

drop cap
A large capital letter used at the start of a paragraph or section of a book. Larger than the surrounding letters, a drop cap is often used as a decorative element.

dummy
A book dummy is a mock-up of a book, complete with the text and images in place. This physical mock-up assists editors, authors, and illustrators, particularly with picture books, and gives a sense of the book's overall design and sequence.

dump
A display unit that holds multiple copies of a title or series. They are either floor displays or countertop displays and are often set up at the checkout counters and referred to as point of purchase displays or "dumps." Retailers must purchase a minimum number of books to get the display and publishers offer incentives for them to do so. For example, a 12-copy display might be offered to the retailer as "buy ten, get two free." These displays are usually made of heavy corrugated cardboard.

duplicate submission
The publication of the same intellectual material more than once by either the author or publisher. This is most often seen in the academic world, when an

author might publish the same study in more than one journal, or submit it to the same journal twice. Not to be confused with multiple submissions or simultaneous submissions.

dust jacket

Also called a jacket, this is the laminated paper wrapping a hardcover book. The flaps of the dust jacket fold into the front and back covers and contain information about the book (front flap) and author (back flap) and often reviews or an excerpt on the back cover.

E

EAN Barcode (European Article Number)

A standardized 13-digit barcode that is used globally to track items sold in the retail market. Magazines use a 12-digit UPC code.

early readers (also known as easy readers or beginning chapter books)

Books aimed at children ages 5–9 who are moving beyond picture books. Early Readers (64 pages) are longer than picture books (32–48 pages) and have text and illustrations on every page. The vocabulary is targeted to the early reader and is intended to help them move on to chapter books.

e-book

The digital book that can be read on a handheld device or computer. Usually spelled ebook without the hyphen.

editor's alteration (EA)

Used when marking a correction made to layouts or proofs by the editor.

e-galleys

Instead of using an ARC or print galley for promotion, an e-galley is the final proof of a title released prior to publication in e-book format to reviewers and targeted readers. NetGalley helps publishers such as Hachette, Penguin Random House, and Simon & Schuster, among others, distribute their e-galleys.

EDItEUR

The trade standards body for the global book, e-book, audiobook and serials supply chains, with over 110 members in 25 countries around the world.

editing

The process of reviewing and making changes to a text in terms of content, structure, and language. Editors plan, review, and revise content for publication.

Electronic Data Interchange (EDI)

Communication of standard business documents between vendor and buyer. Can include Purchase Orders, Purchase Order Acknowledgements, Stock Levels, and Advanced Ship Notices.

electronic rights

The right to publish material in electronic formats, such as e-books.

elevator pitch

A brief and compelling sales pitch to sell a work to a potential buyer done in the time it takes to ride in an elevator, about 30 seconds.

embargo agreement

An agreement that booksellers sign with the publisher to ensure that they cannot sell a book until the on sale date. These books are referred to as embargoed before they have reached their on sale date. When embargoed books are shipped to a bookseller, they are clearly labeled so that bookstores can set those boxes aside and only open and make them available on the actual on sale date. See **strict on sale date**

embossing

Embossing and debossing are the two main forms of stamping that can be used on a book jacket or cover.

Embossing means that the image or text is stamped and appears raised above the rest of the paper on the jacket or cover.

em dash

An em dash is the width of a lowercase "m". The longer em dash (—) is used to mark a break in a sentence or to separate additional information.

en dash

An en dash is the width of a lowercase n. The en dash (–) helps to relate words and numbers and is used instead to mark ranges, for example, "On the Dover–Calais crossing." Not to be confused with the hyphen, which isn't a dash, but a punctuation mark.

end caps

A book stand is usually found at the end of the aisle in most bookstores that provide information about a specific title or titles.

endnote

Part of the back matter, endnotes are citations usually used in academic or scholarly writing. End notes provide additional references or explanations, such as an article, research paper, or book citation at the end of a book chapter or at the end of the book. Endnotes are used if placement in the text is deemed too distracting or inhibits the flow of the text. Endnotes are referenced in the text with a superscript number that relates to their placement in the back matter.

endpaper (or end sheet)

This is the paper glued to the inside of a hardcover case, front and back. Endpapers can be blank, a solid color, or printed in one to four colors.

EPUB

A file format for ebooks that includes the entire publication: HTML files, images, CSS style sheets, and other information, as well as metadata.

eReader

A device (often handheld) that is dedicated to reading ebooks, like a Kindle or Nook.

errata

A loose slip of paper inserted into a printed book that details the corrections to any errors that are in the book.

escalator

A clause in a contract that ties royalty rates to sales, i.e., the royalty rate increases (escalates) depending on the sales.

estimate

An estimate is usually prepared by the manufacturing or production department working with outside vendors to determine the expected cost of a book (paper, print, and bind) and can include design costs and permissions for art or photography for the entire book or just the cover.

evergreen content

Content that continues to provide value to readers no matter when they stumble upon it. The post or article can be referenced long after it was originally published, and even then, it's still valuable to the reader (ex: how-to guides, glossaries, check lists).

exclusive

When an author gives an agent or a publisher (or an agent gives a publisher) a set time to consider acquiring a work without competition from other agents or publishers.

Extensible Markup Language (XML)

A markup language that allows the user to store and transfer data in a shareable way. XML is used for data storage, data exchange, and data management, and is less commonly used for web development.

F

fair use

The right to use copyrighted material without the permission of the copyright owner under the following conditions:

- The Purpose and Character of the Use
- The Nature of the Copyrighted Work.
- The Amount or Substantiality of the Portion Used.
- The Effect of the Use on the Potential Market for or Value of the Work.

fan fiction

Fiction created by non-professionals based on existing properties, usually published online or in fanzines. Some fan fiction is adopted into *original* works successfully, for example, *Fifty Shades of Grey.*

File Transfer Protocol (FTP)

Enables transfer of files between companies. Used for delivery of metadata and ebook files from publisher content systems to data recipients.

film rights

A clause in a book contract that allows for rights (or an option) to be sold to make a movie of a book property.

first pass

A printout or PDF of the first typeset version of a book, which will still need to be proofread and corrected. Often used to print the ARCs and galleys that sales and marketing will use to promote the book.

first print

This is the number of copies a publisher expects to print of a new title.

first serial rights

A book excerpt that is sold to a newspaper, magazine, or periodical for publication prior to the book's publication. Standard contracts usually specify a 90/10 split between the author and the

publisher, but can be negotiated by the agent. See **serial rights**

flap copy

The text on the dust jacket flaps. Usually, a brief description of the book on the front flap, and an author bio and photo on the back flap.

flash fiction

A fiction genre, flash fiction is a short short story of 1500 or fewer words.

flush left or right

Typographic instruction to set the text against the right or left margin.

flyleaf

The flyleaf is an extension of the end-paper that isn't glued to the cover. Like the endpaper or end sheet, it can be blank, a solid color, or printed.

foil stamping

In the printing process, the use of dies to apply foil to a jacket or hardcover book case to create decorative effects.

Folded and Gathered sheets (F&Gs)

These four-color folded and gathered printed sheets are not bound, but loose signatures wrapped with the full jacket (with flaps). Used primarily for children's picture books.

folio

The page number in a printed book.

font

A font is a complete set of characters (letters, numbers, punctuation, symbols, upper and lower case letters) in a particular size and style of type. See **typeface**

footband

Used in hardcover binding, a footband is made from a small strip of material, usually manufactured separately, and placed at the bottom of the book spine. Footbands conceal the glue of the binding and help keep the signatures together, providing structural support for the pages. Also called an endband, it is most effective when sewn in place, but may also be glued for decorative purposes thereby losing its support function. See **headband**

footnote
An explanatory note or reference placed at the bottom of the book page that references it. Footnotes are referenced in the text with a superscript number that corresponds to the citation at the bottom of the page.

For Position Only (FPO)
Low resolution images used to indicate size and placement in a design, but not intended for use in the final product.

foreign rights
The license to publish a book in a different country and language from the original publisher. See **co-edition**

foreword
Part of the front matter of a book, the Foreword is written by someone other than the author and serves as an introduction to a book.

formatting
This refers to the general appearance of the text of a book, including font size, line spacing, paragraph breaks, word count, and page number.

freelancer
An independent contractor who is self-employed and works on a per-job basis for a variety of clients.

French fold
Also known as French flaps or double gate folds. The cover of a paperback is printed on a wider sheet, extending about 3 to 5 inches on each side of the front and back cover panels to create a front and back flap. Handy as a bookmark, they add elegance to a trade paperback.

frequency
The number of times per year that a magazine is published.

frontlist
Frontlist are new titles—the books being published in the current season.

front matter
The first section of a book, front matter includes all the preliminary text for the book and can include the half title page, title page, copyright page, contents page, dedication, preface, foreword, acknowledgements, and reviews. See **Appendix D: Front and Back Matter**

frontispiece
The frontispiece is an illustration that usually faces the title page. Part of the front matter, a frontispiece can be used in both books and magazines.

G

generative AI
A type of machine learning that can generate text, images, video, and other content based on prompts given by a user. Offers further functionality to traditional AI by creating its own patterns.

genre
A specific category of book, such as romance, science fiction, mystery, fantasy, fiction, nonfiction, poetry, horror, and comedy, to name a few.

ghostwriter
Someone who writes under another person's name, based on their ideas and material, without receiving credit or byline.

gloss lamination
A finish for jackets and book covers that adds a layer of plastic coating to the paper, giving it a shiny appearance that enhances the color of the ink.

glossary

Part of the back matter, a glossary is an alphabetical list of terms and their definitions that are specific to the subject of the book.

glued binding

Glued binding can be used with either perfect, burst, or notched signatures. The difference between glued and perfect binding is usually only in the type of glue used. The alternative to glued binding is sewn, which is sturdier and often used for library sales. See **burst binding**, **notch binding**, and **smyth-sewn**

graphic novel

While some might think a graphic novel is a genre, it is considered a format, since they encompass fiction and nonfiction. Like comic books, graphic novels may use text and sequential art to tell a story, but unlike comics, in a much longer page length. Graphic novels may be original works, or collections of previously serialized works.

grid

In graphic design, a grid is a way to organize layouts, i.e., the text and graphic elements on the page. In traditional book and magazine print, there are several different types of grids. A manuscript grid is a one column grid per page used in most books, and baseline grids are evenly spaced horizontal lines like the pages of a notebook, for example.

For digital layouts, grids are dynamic, scaling up and down depending on the digital device. For example, if a digital design is 4-columns on an iPad, it might scale down automatically to 1-column on a phone with a smaller screen.

gutter

In books and magazines: The inner margins of a book page, where the book is bound, i.e., the blank space where the left and right hand pages meet. The gutter is usually blank and must be a certain distance from the binding.

In comics: The space between each of the panels.

H

hairline

Usually refers to a hairline rule, which is the thinnest graphic rule (line) that is printable.

half-bound

Similar to a three-piece case, a half-bound book is bound with leather on the spine that extends to the front and back covers in addition to having the corners bound in leather. Without the corners bound in leather, it is called a quarter bound book. If the leather corners are very wide, it is called a three-quarter bound book.

hard copy

A physical printout of computer or digital text.

hardcover

A book bound with a rigid board, usually cardboard, covered in cloth or paper, that also includes a dust jacket; a format specified in a grant of rights; sometimes called casebound in education markets.

headband

Used in hardcover binding, a headband is made from a small strip of material, usually manufactured separately, and placed at the top of the book spine. Headbands conceal the glue of the binding and help keep the signatures together, providing structural support for the pages. Also called an endband, it is most effective when sewn in place, but may also be glued for decorative purposes, thereby losing its support function. See **footband**

header

A page header appears at the top of a printed page and has information relevant to the book or chapter, often along with a page number. See **running head**

hex (hexadecimal)

A six-digit number used in CSS, HTML, and design software applications to represent color.

high concept

In both fiction and nonfiction, a high concept book is plot driven, is easy to pitch, and has mass commercial appeal. These types of books must be immediately intriguing and unique even before one word of the manuscript is read. See **low concept**

hook

A sales and marketing term that is a condensed sales pitch that gets people interested, i.e., "hooking them in."

house style

A term used for the set of rules or guidelines that a publisher uses for their internal and external communications. These guidelines ensure consistency in grammar, spelling, and other usages.

hybrid press

While a hybrid publisher functions like a traditional publisher in some respects, this publishing model combines elements of self-publishing. In the hybrid model, authors keep more of their rights and greater share of the royalties, but pay some of the production costs and don't receive an advance.

HyperText Markup Language (HTML)

A markup language used to create webpages or web applications. The standard mark-up language for web pages, HTML describes the structure of the content, both in terms of the

text itself and the way each piece of text relates to the other pieces of text on that page.

HyperText Transfer Protocol (HTTP)

A set of rules for transferring data over the web. This includes text, images, sound, video, and other multimedia files. HTTP is the foundation of the World Wide Web and is used to load web pages using hypertext links.

hyphen

A punctuation mark, the hyphen is used to hyphenate words in justified type, compound modifiers, and in phone numbers.

I

imprint

A trade name used by a publisher to brand their works and market to different demographics. A larger company such as Penguin Random House has many publishing groups, such as Random House or The Knopf Doubleday Publishing Group. Each of these, in turn, has their own imprints. For example, within The Knopf Doubleday Publishing Group are the imprints Knopf, Anchor Books, Double Day, Everyman's Library, Nan A. Talese, Pantheon Books, Schocken Books, Vintage Books, and Vintage Español.

independent booksellers

Unlike chain stores, independent booksellers are not owned by large conglomerates, they are small standalone retail stores selling directly to the public.

independent press

A small press that is not a part of a larger corporation.

index

Part of the back matter of a book, the index is a quick reference guide, listing in alphabetical order the names, places, things in the book along with the page numbers where they can be found to help readers easily find information.

indexer

Someone who creates and verifies the index, usually for nonfiction or reference titles.

influencer

In marketing, an influencer is someone who can influence potential buyers by promoting or recommending a book or product on social media. This can be broken down by the number of people an influencer can reach on social media: Nano influencers (1K–10K followers); Micro influencers (10K–100K followers); Macro influencers (100K–1M followers); and Mega or celebrity influencers (1M+ followers).

initial cap

An oversized letter at the beginning of a paragraph, chapter, or in this case, a sentence. See **drop cap**

insertion order

Typically used in advertising, an insertion order is a signed agreement between a publisher and an advertiser that specifically outlines the terms of an ad campaign.

institutional sales

Generally book sales primarily to schools and libraries.

Intellectual Property (IP)

Creative expressions that include literary and artistic works, as well as designs, logos, symbols, names, and images that can be protected by copyright, patents, and trademarks.

Intellectual Property Rights (IPR)

Legal rights given to a creator or inventor to protect their creative expressions.

interior layout

Arranging and formatting text for a book using InDesign or another software program. Layouts include fonts, spacing, the styling of chapter headings, margins, running heads, and page numbers—all the design elements of a book.

International Standard Book Number (ISBN)

An ISBN is a 13-digit number that serves as a product identifier. It is used by publishers, booksellers, libraries, internet retailers, and other supply chain participants for ordering, listing, sales records, and stock control purposes. The ISBN identifies the registrant as well as the specific title, edition, and format.

International Standard Name Identifier (ISNI)

A 16-digit number used to uniquely identify persons and organizations involved in creative activities. Generally this is an author, editor, or other type of book contributor. It can also be applied to public personas, such as pseudonyms, stage names, record labels, or publishing imprints.

International Standard Serial Number (ISSN)

An ISSN is an 8-digit code used to identify newspapers, journals, magazines, and periodicals of all kinds and on all media—print and electronic.

interstitial advertisement

An interstitial ad is a full-screen ad that covers the entire interface of the host app. These ads are designed to be placed between content, and are typically displayed at transition points in an app flow, such as between activities, during a pause, or between levels in a game.

J

joint contract
A book contract with two or more authors (or illustrators) that outlines the division of royalties and all rights.

justify
Used in typography indicating that the line of text is from margin to margin.

K

kerning
The space between letter pairs or individual characters, which can help make the text more readable. Often confused with tracking. See **tracking**

Key Performance Indicator (KPI)
Metric used to measure your progress toward a business goal. In digital publishing, popular KPIs might include clicks, impressions, reach, cost per click, and subscribers.

kill fee
In magazine and book publishing, where a set amount of money is given to a writer, illustrator, or photographer after an article or artwork has been commissioned, but canceled and not used prior to publication.

Knowledge Base (KB)
Central database for libraries that contains bibliographic metadata, links to view full content, subscription licenses, and MARC records. Each library can access the KB and then use the metadata within their local online catalog. This allows the library patrons to link to the resources the library licenses without managing URLs individually by title.

Knowledge Bases And Related Tools (KBART)
A metadata standard for transferring publisher data to library knowledge base services. Often the data includes fields that indicate books sold in publisher library collections.

L

lamination
A process in printing that covers the printed jacket or cover in a protective layer of film made of polypropylene, polyester, or nylon. There are three basic types of lamination: matte, gloss, and silk.

landscape
Formatting a page horizontally so the width is greater than the height.

launch meeting
A launch meeting is a mostly internal meeting (sometimes outsiders such as librarians are invited, too) to announce the upcoming publication list to marketing, sales, and publicity departments.

layouts
In graphic design, layouts refer to the text and images for a book, magazine, or other publication being laid out in page form, with all design elements in place, such as font, margins, title type, running heads, page numbers, and color.

There are different types of layouts in web design:

Fixed-width: Layouts where the width of the entire page has a specific numerical value and stays consistent.

Liquid: Layouts where the width of the entire page is flexible depending on the width of the viewer's browser.

Fluid: Allows you to align elements so that they automatically adjust their alignment and proportions for different page sizes and orientations.

Responsive: Automatically reflows the text to fit the screen on which it is being viewed.

leading

The space between lines of type. The term comes from when text was hand typeset and thin strips of lead were inserted between lines of type to increase the vertical distance between them.

lettering

The typography, principally based on hand-designed fonts and occasionally still executed by hand, of speech and text in print and digital media.

letterspacing

Also known as character spacing, letterspacing is the adjustment of horizontal space between letters in a text block. Unlike kerning, which only affects letter pairs, letterspacing affects all of the letters.

library binding

A binding method with cloth reinforcement, and often a different method of sewing the pages together, that makes a hardcover book more durable and long-lasting. See **smyth sewn**

Library of Congress Classification Number (LCCN)

This is a number used by academic libraries for assigning shelf location for individual books.

Library of Congress Subject Headings (LCSH)

Managed by the Library of Congress, this subject listing is used by library catalogers. Allows for academic libraries to share subject classifications.

license

In any book contract, the author, the holder of the copyright, can grant rights to publish their work or license a publisher to publish their work. In academic or scholarly publishing, the author will either transfer their copyright to the publisher or license the rights for publication, distribution, and use of research.

line break

The way a particular sentence breaks to a new line. Production editors often review line breaks as part of the final stages of book layout, to ensure that the text layout will not distract from the reading experience.

line editing

An editor works line by line to correct or improve the text by tightening sentence structure, reviewing word choices, increasing clarity, and ensuring that the pace and sequence flow smoothly.

list price

Also referred to as the manufacturer's suggested retail price (MSRP); usually the highest price a consumer will pay.

logo

Specially designed typographical or hand-lettered symbol, text, or design that is used to identify an organization, product, or brand.

Lorum Ipsum

Dummy text used as a placeholder in the graphic, print, and publishing industries for previewing layouts and visual mockups.

low concept

A low concept book is generally fiction that is character-driven, not easily explained, and addresses everyday life issues and relationships. See **high concept**

M

Machine Readable Cataloging (MARC)

The metadata schema used by libraries to create catalog entries.

managing editor (ME)

Organizes all departments' efforts, coordinating a schedule for the entire list of upcoming publications to ensure deadlines and budgets are met. The Managing Editor works with a staff of Production Editors (either in-house or freelance) who do the copyediting and proofreading and are responsible for keeping a title on schedule. The Managing Editor plans a publication's budget and communicates with editors, art directors, marketing, and sales, as well as outside vendors to ensure the publication meets deadlines and quality standards.

manga

The Japanese form of comics (also MANHWA in Korea).

manifest

A list of the contents of a package. In the context of ebooks, the manifest lists everything contained inside a digital book package (like an EPUB file). See **Open Package Format (OPF)**

manual buys

In this process, advertisers purchase ad space from a publisher directly without the use of AdTech platforms.

manuscript (MS)

The text of the book as the author gives it to the publisher. Usually, it has already undergone a round of editing with the author's agent and will undergo further editing with the publisher.

marketing

A function and department that helps the various sales departments (includes special sales and library sales) get a book to distributors, bookstore buyers, and other channels. Marketers create and implement marketing plans that can include advertising, sales materials, point-of-sale displays, and social media. See **Appendix A: Elements of A Marketing Kit**

marketing plan

A marketing plan outlines the marketing strategies for promoting a specific book, author, or series to drive sales.

mass market

A relatively inexpensive paperback book measuring 4.25 x 6.87 inches. Mass market paperbacks are generally sold not only in bookstores, but grocery stores and airports and are less expensive than trade paperbacks.

masthead

Used in magazine publications, it is a one page or one-column list of everyone involved in the magazine's creation. It includes editorial staff, publisher, contact information, and other information about the publication.

matte lamination

Unlike gloss lamination, matte lamination is not shiny; it adds a flat and velvety appearance to a jacket or book cover.

mechanical binding

A book block is drilled to allow the placement of a binding material of some kind. Spiral Bound Notebooks are a common example of mechanical binding.

mechanicals (also called paste-up or artwork boards)

This is a term that was once essential in publishing and is now outdated, but still used. Mechanicals were illustration boards printed with a non-reproducing blue ink to indicate where text and images would go. They were larger than the final size of the printed work and used to create the hardcopy layouts of a work that would be photographed to create the film used to print the work. Text would be generated by a typesetting machine and output into repros (reproduction proofs that are clear and sharp and that serve as photographic copy for a printing plate) that would be glued or waxed onto the board. Artwork would also be pasted down with the text—a halftone piece of art would be photocopied and pasted onto the board with the letters FPO across it, meaning it was "For Position Only". At the printer, the real artwork would be photographed and cut into the final film. Any piece of line art would be pasted down onto the board and shot with the text. Now, these layouts are created on the computer with greater accuracy.

media buyer
The person who oversees the media buying for a company, the media buyer negotiates with different media channels to purchase ad space and time.

media planning
A process where media planners work to identify the target audience, conduct market research, establish goals, and determine a budget for their product, service, or brand on multiple media platforms.

memoir
A nonfiction narrative of a person's life written in the first person; a personal or family history.

metadata
When it comes to book publishing and marketing, metadata are the vital details about a book that allow distributors and retailers to easily identify what it's about and successfully market it. According to the Book Industry Study Group, metadata includes information such as page count and critical reviews, title, author, or series.

middle grade
Books for readers ages 8–12, grades 3 through 6, generally 30,000–50,000 words in length that don't include profanity, graphic violence, or sexuality.

midlist
Books that aren't bestsellers, but sell reasonably well. Midlist books on a publishers publication list will have projected sales that are moderate, but not expected to be a bestseller.

model release
A binding legal document signed by the subject of a photograph giving a photographer or publisher permission to publish it.

monochrome
Made with a single color or hue, a monochrome can be a photograph or picture, printed or appearing in black and white or in different tones of only one color.

monograph
A scholarly piece of writing, often book length, that is highly detailed and thoroughly documented on a specific subject or field of inquiry.

multiple submission
These are manuscript submissions made simultaneously by an author to more than one agent or publisher, or by an agent to more than one publisher. Some agents and publishers do not accept multiple submissions. See **simultaneous submission**

N

National Information and Standards Organization (NISO)
An organization which identifies, develops, maintains, and publishers technical standards and best practices to manage information. Many of their guidelines focus on the needs of the book and journal industries.

Natural Language Processing (NLP)
Machine learning technology that allows computers to understand and interpret human language.

net royalty
When the author's share of royalties is based on the publisher's net revenue, which is usually less than a royalty based on the retail price. See **royalties**

newsstand sales
Magazines sold through newsstand outlets. See **single-copy sales**

niche marketing
When the marketing and promotional efforts for a book are directed to a specific group of buyers, either by geographic location or those with a specific interest. Although niche titles can be sold nationally, they are often sold through specialized retail outlets.

non-exclusive
Copyright holders may choose to grant some rights – such as those for second serials or for sales in the open market territory – to more than one party.

nonfiction
A genre of literature that is intended to inform or educate readers, these books are based on facts and real events or people.

non-returnable
Books that cannot be returned to the publisher if they haven't been sold. Most bookstores work on being able to return books to the publishers, but some accounts aren't allowed to do so, i.e., non-returnable.

notch binding
In this type of binding, the signatures are gathered and a deep, square notch is cut across the spine at intervals of an inch or so. This exposes the leaves of all the pages in the signature and ensures even adhesive application. See **burst binding, glued binding**, and **smyth-sewn**

novelty book
Books for children that include special elements such as pop-ups, lift-the-flap, hidden audio chips, or fold-out pages.

O

offset printing (also called offset lithography)
Widely used printing technique in which the inked image on a printing plate is printed on a rubber cylinder and then transferred (i.e., offset) to paper or other material.

Online Information Exchange (ONIX)
Metadata schema used by publishers to supply bibliographic metadata to retailers, aggregators, and libraries.

on sale date
The date that a magazine issue of a given title or a book title is scheduled to be put up on display in retail outlets.

opacity
In referencing CSS, opacity is the degree to which content is hidden behind an element.

In graphic design and photography, opacity is the extent to which something blocks light. How much light passes through an object determines the opacity or transparency: when less light can pass through, the opacity is high and the object appears more solid; when more light can pass through, the opacity is low and the object appears more transparent. See **transparency**

Open Access (OA)
Open Access books and journals are on the rise in academic publishing. These books, chapters, or articles are made available to readers at no charge. Funding for the publication is

often supplied by universities, research centers, foundations, or government agencies.

OpenAI

The company that developed ChatGPT, OpenAI is a research company that is committed to developing and promoting artificial intelligence.

Open Package Format (OPF)

A type of markup language that expresses the relationships between files within an EPUB. This important file contains rules for describing the contents of an EPUB file, the book reading order, and more.

Optical Character Recognition (OCR)

Computer technology that scans text and replicates it into an editable computer file.

option clause

In a publishing contract, an option clause grants the publisher the right to have the opportunity to publish the author's next work at a later time. A "first look" grants the publisher a right to review and make an offer on the author's next work before any other publisher; "topping" gives the publisher a right to acquire rights in the next work by offering a set percentage more than the best offer the author received for the next work.

ORCID (Open Researcher and Contributor ID)

A digital identifier that gives individual researchers the ability to create, manage, and control the visibility of their data or to delegate the data management to their university or another third party.

ornament

Refers to a type ornament that can be used to add space between sections of a text or end a chapter.

is an example of a type ornament. The design firm, Pentagram, created and produced *The Little Book of Typographic Ornament*, a celebration of these graphic decorations, which includes examples from 1700 to the present day.

orphan

A single word at the bottom of a text paragraph.

out-of-print

When a publisher no longer has any copies of a particular title to sell and has no plans to reprint it, the book can be considered out-of-print, which in most cases, means the rights to the title will revert back to the author.

overrun

Publishers often print a slightly larger quantity of books to account for any spoilage that may occur during printing. Most publishers overrun their book jackets so that returned books that have a damaged cover can be re-jacketed and sold. See **spoilage, underrun**

Oxford comma

Also known as a serial comma, it is a comma most often found in trade books that appears before the "and" in a series of items, for example: Books, magazines, and other media.

Newspapers do not use the Oxford comma, since that extra comma takes up too much space, so generally: Books, magazines and other media.

P

packager

A book packager conceives of a book project, hires authors and illustrators, and pays them a flat fee. The book packager then sells the project to a publishing house. In some cases a large publisher will hire a book packager to develop a project, hire the writers and illustrators, and deliver the final project to the publisher.

page break
The way text breaks from one page to the next. Production editors often review page breaks as part of the final stages of book layout, to check for things like widows and orphans, and ensure that the text layout will not distract from the reading experience.

page count
The total number of pages in a printed work. Every sheet of paper counts as two pages.

palette
A word associated with art and color, it also can refer to a specific set of colors. See **color palette**

panel
The integral unit of comics storytelling, a single frame.

Pantone Matching System (PMS)
This is a proprietary numbering system for colors from the Pantone company. This system standardizes 1,114 colors by assigning each a number. This provides consistency to the colors used for any specific book or company.

Paper, Printing, and Binding (PP&B)
The costs for creating the physical print copy of a book: paper, print, and binding.

paperback or perfect bound book
A standard binding for paperbacks that uses glue to hold the text block to the cover; a format specified in a grant of rights.

Paper-over-board (POB)
In book production, a paper-over-board is a hardcover book without a dust jacket. Instead, the printed cover is glued to the hardcover board.

peer review
When publishing academic journals and scholarly texts, it is important to have the scientific, scholarly, or professional work reviewed by peers, i.e., individuals with similar academic standing in the same field.

pen name
The name a writer or author uses instead of their real name. Also called a nom de plume or a pseudonym. Examples include: John Le Carré, the pen name of David Cornwell; Joyce Carol Oates who used the pen name Rosamund Smith; and Elena Ferrante, the pen name of an author whose name is still unknown to her readers.

periodical
A magazine or newspaper published at regular intervals, daily, weekly, and monthly, for example.

permissions
It is necessary to obtain a signed permission from the copyright holder in order to include a quote, poem, photo, song, logo, illustration, map, or excerpt from their creative work in another publication. The permissions form is a legal document that outlines the exact terms of the use – one-time only, for example, or inclusion in all editions of the work.

physical proof (also called a hard proof)
Usually created by the printer, a physical proof can be bound or unbound and provides the publisher (or author) with an exact copy of the final book to review before the first print run.

pica
A typographic unit of measure corresponding to approximately 1/6 of an inch, or from 1/68 to 1/73 of a foot. One pica is further divided into 12 points.

picture book
Books that are written for young children between the ages of 5 and 8 using words and picture (and sometimes only images) to tell a story. Typically 32, 40 or 48 pages in length.

pixel
Derived from the words "picture element," it is the smallest element in a computer display. The number of pixels determines the resolution of an image – the more pixels, the sharper the image. Numbers that reference resolution are usually written this way: 1920 x 1080 and reference the number of horizontal (1920) and vertical (1080) pixels.

plant
Plant is the term on the P&L that encapsulates all the fixed, one-time costs that go into the production of a book. These might include composition, design, copyediting, etc. See **Profit and Loss Statement (P&L)**

platform
This refers to an author's ability to reach an audience and market their work. It could include their social media presence, blog, web site, publishing history, and speaking experience.

podcast
A word derived from iPod and broadcast, a podcast is a digital audio or video file that can be downloaded to a mobile device or computer over the internet. It typically consists of a series of episodes that cover various topics, such as news, storytelling, interviews, educational content, or entertainment.

point
The smallest unit of measure in typography, used for measuring font size.

Point-of-Sale (POS)
The point at which a purchase is made. POS refers to the payment counter in a retail store or the payment page for an online purchase.

portrait
Formatting a page vertically so the height is greater than the width.

preface
Part of the front matter, a preface is usually written by the author and is a personal note that might include the author's experience writing the book, the purpose of the book, the writing process, or how to use the book.

prepress
All of the steps required to prepare a book to be sent to the printer.

press or media kit
A package of information sent or given to members of the media to promote a publication or company. In book publishing, a press or media kit includes a press release, author bio and photo, book covers, product information, book excerpt, and other materials. See **Appendix B: Elements of a Press or Media Kit**

press release
A statement sent to media outlets from the publisher announcing a new publication (book or periodical). See **Appendix C: Elements of a Press Release**

primary rights
Rights held by the author that are transferred to the publisher. Essentially, the right to publish the manuscript in print and electronic formats.

Print on Demand (POD)
Using digital technology, a system that prints smaller quantities of books than a traditional printer. Also known as Print to Order (PTO).

print run
The number of copies of a book produced at one time. An initial print run

is the number of copies the publisher has printed for the initial release/publication of the book.

printer
A company that prints the interior pages of the book and the cover. Often, the printer is also the binder.

printer's errors
These are any mistakes made by the printer during the manufacturing process and can include smudges, ink blots, incorrectly bound pages, or other errors introduced by the printer. These errors must be corrected, but the printer cannot charge the publisher for correcting them.

production editor
Also called a production manager, the production editor coordinates the process that brings an edited manuscript to completion as a finished, printed book, overseeing the copyediting and proofreading, reviewing layouts and proofs, and making sure the title adheres to deadlines.

Profit and Loss Statement (P&L)
Profit and Loss statements analyze the cost of a book (production, art, and editorial costs) against potential income and include all the relevant data such as retail price, royalty, quantity, and overhead to predict profitability.

programmatic buys
A media buying method that uses specific software to automatically bid on ad space, based on consumer profiles.

proofs
The purpose of a proof is to check for any typos or formatting errors. A proof copy of a book includes the cover and interiors and is sent by the printer to the publisher for a final review. Usually the final stage before printing.

proofreading
In book publishing, this is generally the last step in the editorial process after editing and copyediting. Proofreading is the final read of the layouts and focuses on minor inconsistencies such as typos and grammatical mistakes.

psychographics
The study of consumers and grouping them into market segments based on their psychological makeup, including values, attitudes, personality, and lifestyle.

public domain
Not protected by copyright and available for use by the general public. A work in the public domain either has never been protected by copyright, or the copyright has lapsed or expired.

publication date
The date on which a book or periodical is scheduled to be published.

publicity
Getting media attention for a book through newspapers, TV shows, radio, podcasts, social media, or events.

publisher
Any company (or individual) that prepares and issues printed works such as books or periodicals for sale and distribution.

pullquote
Sentences from the text that are set in a larger font across columns of text. More often used in periodicals or nonfiction books.

Purchase Order (PO)
A legal and binding document that a buyer sends to a vendor to authorize a purchase. It includes quantity and price and all of the details of the transaction.

Purchase Order Acknowledgement (POA)

Confirmation from the vendor that the order was received, the amount of stock that will be shipped, and the date it will be shipped.

Q

QR code

A Quick Response code is a type of two-dimensional barcode that provides easy access to online information through the digital camera on a smartphone or tablet.

query letter

A letter sent by an author to an agent or editor pitching their book to elicit interest in their work. A query letter must have a "hook" that will spark the reader's interest, along with the title, subtitle, information about the book's author, genre or category, and a word count.

R

raster

Raster graphics are digital images made up of pixels, each with its own color value. Raster graphics are good for capturing photographs, but when scaled up or printed at a large size, they might become pixelated or indistinct. See **vector**

rate base

In magazine publishing, rate base indicates the circulation figure the publisher uses to calculate advertising rates. Essentially, the number of subscribers to a given publication.

reach

The total number of different people or households in a target audience who are exposed to an ad.

readers report

An important tool used by literary agents and editors, it is a one-page synopsis of a book with a recommendation to acquire or pass, usually written by an assistant or associate editor.

Really Simple Syndication (RSS) also known as Rich Site Summary

A technology used to distribute frequently updated content, such as news articles, blog posts, or podcasts, in a standardized format. The purpose of RSS is to allow users to subscribe to these updates and receive them in a centralized location, often referred to as an "RSS feed reader" or "RSS aggregator."

recto

The right-hand page of an open book. See **verso**

redundant publication

Used in academic publishing, this occurs when one study is divided into different parts and submitted to two or more journals without cross-referencing, justification, or permission. Self-plagiarism is one form of redundant publication, where an author uses content from previous works without proper citation or reference to the original work.

Reinforcement Learning with Human Feedback (RLHF)

An additional layer of training that uses human feedback to help ChatGPT learn to follow directions and generate responses that are satisfactory to humans.

reissue

When a title hasn't been available for some period of time and is out of print and the publisher reissues it. When a title is out of print, an author may ask for the rights back. In this situation, the publisher either reissues the book and retains the rights, or reverts the rights back to the author.

remainder copies
Trade books in the United States that are sold in retail outlets can be returned to the publisher. If a book doesn't sell well, the publisher can sell off their inventory (and free up warehouse space) at a greatly reduced price.

reprint
When the copies of a book have sold out of the print run, a publisher reprints the work.

reprint rights
The legal right to reprint or reproduce a work, including the text, illustrations, or photographs that have already been published. Reprint rights can be for the entire book or an excerpt. Second serial rights are a type of reprint right.

resolution
The sharpness or clarity of an image. Resolution refers to the visual quality of an image or photograph, i.e., the number of pixels. In printing, resolution is expressed as dots per inch (DPI). The smaller and finer the dots, the higher the DPI and the sharper the printout. With displays and digital images, resolution is expressed as PPI (pixels per inch). See **Dots Per Inch**

returns
In book publishing: Brick and mortar stores will not order a book unless it is returnable; this means if a book doesn't sell, it can be returned to the publisher. Upon return of the full book or cover, the bookseller will receive a credit for the amount they paid for the book.

In magazine publishing: In single-copy sales, magazines that are distributed but not sold. In many cases, unsold copies are returned to the wholesaler, who processes and records them, issues credit records, shreds the copies, and verifies, by affidavit, that the returns have been destroyed.

RGB (Red Green Blue)
A system that represents the colors used on a digital display screen. Red, green, and blue can be combined to make millions of colors. RGB is the color system best suited for digital designs, while CMYK is used for printed images. See **CMYK**

royalties
The amount a publisher pays an author for the rights to publish their book. Royalty rates vary for different formats, i.e., hardcover, paperback, e-book, and audio, for example). Royalties are usually based on a percentage of the retail price ranging from 7½% for a paperback and 10-15% for a hardcover. See **net royalty**

RSS Aggregator
Also known as an RSS reader or feed reader, an RSS Aggregator is a software or web-based tool that gathers and displays content from various RSS feeds in a centralized location.

running head
Also known as a page header, a running head appears at the top of a page, separated from the main text and can include the title of a book (or abbreviated title), chapter title (or abbreviated chapter title), author, and page number. Running heads differ depending on whether they appear on the right or left-hand side of the page.

s

saddle stitch
A type of binding in which the pages are first folded and then stapled together at the fold.

sales call
Publisher's sales reps have regular appointments to meet with bookstore buyers to pitch their front list titles.

sales conference

Where editors and publishers present their new titles for the coming season to the sales, marketing, and publicity departments.

sales kit

Sales kits can include different types of samples and promotional materials such as covers, ARCs, BLADs, and F&Gs.

sales rep

Sales representatives can either be commissioned sales reps or company sales reps. Commissioned reps work for several different publishers and solicit bookstores and other retail outlets to sell their books. The company reps only sell their company's titles.

sans serif

A typeface without a serif, such as Verdana. From *sans*, the French word for without. Typically, sans serif typefaces have larger x heights than serif typefaces and are a more modern typographic form. Arial is another example of a sans serif font. See **serif, x-height**

Schema.org

Webpage markup with book properties to facilitate better SEO and to improve SERPs.

School Rights Only (SRO)

A grant of rights in a contract that covers the sales to schools.

script

Script typefaces are fonts or type based upon historical or modern handwriting styles.

Search Engine Optimization (SEO)

The practice of optimizing websites and web pages for discovery in search engines and, as a result, more visible placement on search engine results pages.

Search Engine Results Pages (SERP)

The paid and organic results received from a search engine. A publisher can increase its SERP ranking by using SEO. Ranking high on search engines like Google can lead to new prospects, increased traffic, and increased revenue.

second serial rights

A book excerpt that is sold to a newspaper, magazine, or periodical for publication after the book's publication. Standard contracts usually specify a 50/50 split between the author and the publisher, but can be negotiated by the agent. See **serial rights**

self publishing

When an author publishes their work independently at their own expense. All aspects of the publishing process can be done solely by the author or they might hire companies to assist with various aspects of editing, production, marketing, and distribution. See **vanity press**

sell-in

This is a term used by the sales department and means selling into a bookstore or other distributor. It means making the book available to the consumer through a retail outlet. The sales department is responsible for selling-in.

sell sheet

An important sales tool, a sell sheet is a flyer or one-page description of a book that provides all of the essential details about it, including ISBN, retail price, author bio, trim size, and contact information for the publisher. The sell sheet is used to sell or promote a book to retailers and wholesalers. A good sell sheet should be concise, easy to read, and visually compelling.

sell-through

In magazine publishing: also called efficiency or efficiency level. The percentage of distributed newsstand copies that were actually sold.

In book publishing: Selling through to the consumer. Selling-in to a bookstore is great because the book is then available to the consumer, but if they don't buy it, then there's no "sell-through" and books are returned to the publisher. The marketing department is responsible for sell-through.

sensitivity reader
The use of a pre-publication reader of a specific group to identify material which may be deemed problematic.

serial fiction
Books that are published as a series, such as Armistead Maupin's *Tales of the City* or Sue Grafton's Kinsey Millhone books, or a children's series such as Harry Potter or A Series of Unfortunate Events.

serial rights
The right to publish an excerpt from a book usually sold by the book publisher to a magazine or newspaper or other serial publication. Revenue from serial rights is typically split between the author and the publisher according to the contract. First serial rights, when an excerpt is published prior to the book's publication date, are usually split 90% to the author and 10% to the publisher and second serial rights, excerpts published after the book's publication, are split 50/50.

serif
A small line or wedge attached to the end of a letter in a family of fonts. It is also the collective name for typefaces that use serifs, a more ornate letterform. Examples of a serif font include Times Roman or Georgia. There are several different types of serif, including gothic, glyphic, bracketed, oldstyle, wedge, hairline, slab, and more.

sheet-fed
Printed on a press that prints in sheet form as opposed to web-fed, which prints on a continuous roll of paper. See **web-fed**

show card
A printed or hand-lettered card that contains information about a specific book or author. A show card is placed in a bookstore window or close to a display to promote retail sales or an event.

sidebar
Text that is set as a boxed element or column that includes information or emphasizes an aspect of the text. Used in books and periodicals.

signature
In the printing process, signatures are created by paper being printed on both sides and then folded so the pages are in order. See a signature layout (below). Signatures are in configurations of 16 or 32 pages in book publishing and 24 pages in magazine publications. Printers use this type of layout on a press sheet so that after folding the pages are in the correct order. For saddle-stitched booklets, a signature cannot have fewer than 4 pages.

Example of a 16-page Signature

Pg 5	Pg 12	Pg 9	Pg 8
Pg 4	Pg 13	Pg 16	Pg 1

Front of Sheet

Pg 7	Pg 10	Pg 11	Pg 6
Pg 2	Pg 15	Pg 14	Pg 3

Back of Sheet

simultaneous submission

When a literary agent submits a manuscript to more than one publisher. Or when an author submits a manuscript to more than one literary agent. Not to be confused with multiple submissions, which happens in periodical publishing, when more than one piece of work is being submitted, i.e., 3–5 poems or 2–3 short stories.

single-copy sales

Also called newsstand sales. Single copies of magazines sold at retail. Most single-copy sales are made in supermarkets and other mass retail outlets. Many publishers also distribute through specialty stores.

single-source workflow

A type of production workflow where all book output formats (print PDF, ebook, web, etc.) are created simultaneously from a single source text file (often an XML or Microsoft Word file). These workflows typically rely heavily on scripts and automation to generate the book output files.

slush pile

Unsolicited query letters and manuscripts; i.e., a pile of submissions.

smyth-sewn (also known as section sewn)

The sturdiest method of binding a hardcover book with the folded signatures being sewn together at the fold. Also considered "library binding" because of its durability. Smyth sewn books are additionally reinforced with fabric backing and adhesive. The folded and sewn signatures are gathered and sewn together to form a book block. See **burst binding**, **glued binding**, and **notch binding**

special sales

An additional way to sell books, apart from bookstore sales. Special Sales include gift shops and catalogs, as well as other non-bookstore venues such as offices, schools, hospitals, seminars, libraries, or associations.

spine

That area of a book's binding which is visible when a book is shelved in a bookcase; the portion which is attached at the joints to the front and rear covers.

splash

The use of a full page panel in comics.

spoilage

The waste or loss of material during the manufacturing process. In printing, it refers to paper waste, which printers generally estimate to be about ten percent. See **overrun, underrun**

spread

Two facing pages: one left-hand (verso) page and one-right-hand (recto) page.

Standard Account Number (SAN)

A seven-digit code assigned to publishers, bookstores, and distributors and others that signifies a specific address. SANs lessen billing errors and errors in payments and returns.

stet

A directive from a proofreader, copyeditor, editor, or author to cancel an alternation in the text that was previously requested. The word stet comes from the Latin, "let it stand."

strict on sale date

The on sale date refers to the date when a particular book or magazine will go on sale. Strict on sale means that there may be penalties if a bookseller makes the book available to customers before the on sale date. Publishers like on sale dates because it ensures a fair bookselling environment for all stores across the country.

Publishers also like to maintain a uniform release date for a book title because their marketing and promotion efforts are tied to a specific date. Think Harry Potter. See **embargo agreement**

structural edits
Edits made to the overall structure of the work, including plot, organization, character development, scope, or audience.

style sheets
There are two types of style sheet, but both are used to maintain consistency. A style sheet can be created by a copyeditor to ensure that there is consistency in the treatment of numbers, for example, or to note any spelling preferences. Style sheets can also be created by the book designer to ensure consistency in page size, margins, text font and size, headlines, bylines, and other elements of the layout.

sub-agent
Literary agents use other agents to sell subsidiary rights such as movie rights or foreign rights. A literary agent might have a sub-agent in a particular country who helps them sell rights in that country.

subsidiary rights
An author can grant these rights to a publisher or keep them for themselves or any combination of the two. Sub rights typically include foreign rights, permissions, licensing, film and television rights, audio, merchandising, and book club rights.

supply chain
A complex network of suppliers, manufacturers, distributors, and retailers that transforms raw materials into a finished product and delivers it to the consumer.

Supply Side Platform (SSP)
An advertising technology platform that helps publishers and digital media companies sell ad space.

synopsis
A brief summary of a book.

T

Table of Contents (TOC)
An outline, in sequence, of the contents of the book, found at the beginning of a book in the front matter. The table of contents lists chapter and/or section titles.

tail
In comics, the pointer from a balloon to the character speaking.

target audience
Target audiences can be defined by their demographic, psychographic, geographic, and behavioral attributes. These are specific groups of people to whom an advertising message is aimed.

tear sheet
In magazines and newspapers, a tear sheet is proof that an ad has been published. In the past, tear sheets (also called clips) were copies of an ad, "torn" from a publication, to prove to the advertiser that their ad was published. Currently, the industry standard is now electronic, an e-sheet.

tech stack
The various technologies that are used to create ay application. A tech stack includes programming languages, APIs, databases, and front-and back-end tools.

template
A template shows all of the formatting, styles, and dimensions of a given project so there is consistency in the layout. Templates can be created in a variety of different software programs, including Microsoft Word and Adobe InDesign.

territory

The countries where a publisher can sell and distribute a work. In the US, these are:

US or North America: English language rights for the US and Canada

World English: English language rights in the UK, Australia, New Zealand, South Africa. India can sometimes also be included.

World All Languages: Also known as Translation rights, this gives the publisher the right to publish or license the publication throughout the world in any language.

thema

This international subject scheme allows for the assignment of codes and qualifiers to describe the content of the book. Multiple language translations of the codes are available. BISAC regularly updates its mapping to THEMA.

three-piece case

While most hardcover cases are made from one piece of cloth or cover material, a 3-piece case has a spine usually covered in cloth or a cloth equivalent and the front and back panels covered with paper. The cloth spine extends onto the front and back covers.

thumbnails

A smaller version of a layout that can assist in organizing the sequence of pages.

tip sheet

Tip sheets provide bullet points of information about a title to help sales and marketing get the book into the right demographic. Tip sheets will highlight a book's theme or message, content, author information, or anecdotes.

title page

Part of the front matter, the title page is a right-hand that includes the book title, subtitle, author's name, publisher, and the city where the book was published.

to come (TK)

Abbreviation for "to come," used as a placeholder because the letter combination "tk" rarely appears otherwise in the English language.

track changes

This feature in Microsoft Word gives authors and editors a method of collaborating during the editing process. The author can accept or reject an editor's changes to the manuscript and add their own comments.

tracking

A term often confused with kerning (two characters only), used in typography to make type more readable by equally letter spacing an entire sentence or paragraph or whatever copy is selected. See **kerning**

trade book

Books that are available in bookstores and are of general interest to the reading public.

trade paperback

Larger than mass market paperback books and usually printed on heavier paper stock for the interior and the cover. Trade paperbacks are often the same size as the hardcover edition and use the same cover design. These books are usually bound only with glue.

translation rights

Part of foreign rights, these are rights that can be granted by the copyright holder or the publisher to have the work translated into another language (other than the original) and published in another country.

transparency

In graphic design and photography, how much light passes through an object determines its opacity or transparency. When more light can pass through, the opacity is low and the object appears more transparent. When less light passes through, the opacity is high and the object appears more solid. See **opacity**

trim size
The height and width of a book after it has been printed and trimmed in the printing process.

typeface
A typeface includes a series of fonts – roman, bold, italic, condensed, among others. For example Garamond Bold, Garamond Italic, and Garamond Roman are considered to be one typeface, but three fonts. There are three main categories for typefaces: serif, sans serif, and script.

typesetting
The process of setting text into type in a form ready for print and ebook production using different fonts. Typesetting incorporates kerning, line spacing, column width and depth, and other design considerations.

typo
A mistake, such as a misspelled word, in printed text.

typographic hierarchy
Typographic hierarchy consist of three elements: headline, subhead, and text. They create contrast between these elements and make the text more readable. This hierarchy of text (including size, font, color, capital/lowercase letters, bold or italics) highlights the relative importance of the information presented.

typography
The style and appearance of typeset text on a page. Typography involves font style, appearance, and structure to facilitate legibility and visual appeal.

U

underrun
Despite a publisher's order for a certain number of books to be printed, if there is excessive spoilage or printer's errors, the publisher may receive fewer than the number of copies they ordered.

Unique Visitors Per Month (UVPM)
A website metric that shows the total of unique visits to a web site, not counting subsequent visits.

Universal Product Code (UPC)
The barcode on products that allows retailers to automatically record the sale of those products. Magazines are assigned a unique number, which is the last five digits of the UPC. The number allows retail scanners to automatically input a magazine's price and allows wholesaler equipment to identify the publication sold and process returns. Books use an EAN barcode.

unsolicited manuscript
A manuscript that is submitted to an agent or publisher without being requested. See **slush pile**

User-Generated Content (UGC)
Unpaid content produced by users or fans of a product that includes, reviews, blog posts, images, videos. UGC includes work posted to social media platforms, as well as that posted to websites such as Archive of Our Own or Webtoons, where individuals are incited to produce content at their own risk and expenses, in hopes of payment or simply sharing their work with like-minded persons.

User Interface (UI)
The point at which a person and a device, webpage, or app interact. User interfaces enable users to control the computer or device they are interacting

with. User interface components include input and navigation controls, informational components, and containers that keep related material together. These interfaces can include a button, or a drop down menu.

UV coating

A cost-effective option for coating book jackets, ultraviolet coating provides a glossy shine to the jacket or cover and inhibits the paper from curling.

UX writing

Writing that seeks to improve the user experience of a web site, product, or service. UX writing serves as a guide for the user while interacting with a web site or mobile app.

V

vanity press (also known as a subsidy publisher)

A publishing company where anyone can have their book published at their own expense. Unlike self-publishing, vanity presses can provide some design or editorial work in addition to having the book printed.

vector

Two ways of creating digital images are raster and vector. In vector, graphics are made of mathematical equations that define lines, shapes, and curves. Vector graphics can be sized up or down without losing resolution. See **raster**

verso

The left-hand page of an open book. See **recto**

video ads

These are ads inserted into videos, before (pre-roll), in the middle (mid-roll), or after the video completes playback (post-roll). Video ads range in length from 10 to 15 seconds to three minutes. YouTube and Snapchat are two popular venues for video ads.

W

watermark

A faint logo or mark on paper that identifies the maker and is added during the manufacturing process; usually a watermark is barely visible, but is especially notable when the paper is held against the light.

web accessibility

Technology that enables users with disabilities to access and interact with content on a website or in an ebook, regardless of their level of ability or circumstances. These tools can include text transcripts, adding captions, providing an audio or text description for a video, adding special metadata, considering color contrast, and more.

web-fed

A printing press that uses paper in large rolls and prints a continuous sheet that is later collated, folded, and cut.

website

A group of related web pages that are linked together under a single domain name, usually maintained by a company, organization, or individual.

wholesalers

Companies that purchase large quantities of books at a high discount from publishers and then sell them to bookstores and libraries at a lesser discount. Two leading book wholesalers are Baker & Taylor and Ingram Book Group.

In Books: Book wholesalers will purchase books either from the publisher or their distributor in order to supply retailers and libraries with a bundle of books from many different publishers. A library wholesaler may perform added duties of cataloging, labeling, and barcoding books to make them shelf ready for a library.

In Magazines: The companies that physically distribute magazines to single-copy retail outlets, process returns and engage in marketing and in-store service. Wholesalers once served specific geographic territories, But due to retail chains' insistence, one or two major wholesalers are now responsible for magazine distribution to an entire retail chain, whatever the geographic location.

widow
In typesetting, a widow is a single line of text with one or more words that appears at the top of a page or column.

word count
The number of words appearing in a given text. Word counts are important in order to calculate the ultimate page length from manuscript to printed page.

work for hire
A work for hire means that the creator isn't necessarily the copyright owner. Publishers often hire writers and pay a flat fee for the work, not a royalty, and the publisher holds the copyright, not the author. According to the US Copyright Office, "Whether a work is a work made for hire is determined by facts in existence at the time the work is created. There are two situations in which a work made for hire is produced:

(1) when the work is created by an employee as part of the employee's regular duties and (2) when a certain type of work is created as a result of an express written agreement between the creator and a party specially ordering or commissioning the work. When a work is produced under these conditions, the employer or the party ordering or commissioning the work is considered the author and copyright owner. The work made for hire concept

can be complicated and has serious consequences for both the individual who creates a work and the hiring party who is considered to be the author and copyright owner of that work."

X

x-height
The height of the lowercase letter x in a font.

XML
See **Extensible Markup Language**

Y

Young Adult (YA)
A genre of children's books written for children aged 12 to 18.

COMMON TERMS
IN
ARTIFICIAL
INTELLIGENCE

adversarial networks

A concept in machine learning where two models, typically neural networks, compete with each other. This setup enables the generation of new, synthetic instances of data that can pass for real data.

agents

Autonomous entities in AI that perceive their environment and make decisions to maximize their chance of achieving specific goals.

Artificial Intelligence (AI)

A field of computer science dedicated to creating systems capable of performing tasks that require human intelligence. These tasks include learning from experience, understanding natural language, recognizing patterns, and making decisions.

Artificial Neural Network (ANN)

A framework for machine learning algorithms based on a simplified model of human brain function, which can recognize patterns and interpret sensory data.

chatbots

Programs powered by AI designed to interact with humans in their natural languages. These interactions can be via text or speech.

classification

A supervised machine learning technique where an algorithm learns from the training data input to it and uses this learning to classify new observations.

clustering

An unsupervised machine learning technique that groups a set of objects in such a way that objects in the same group (or cluster) are more similar to each other than to those in other groups.

computer vision

An interdisciplinary field that deals with how computers can gain high-level understanding from digital images or videos. It seeks to automate tasks that the human visual system can do.

Convolutional Neural Network (CNN)

A class of deep, feed-forward artificial neural networks most commonly applied to analyzing visual imagery.

data augmentation

Techniques in machine learning for increasing the amount of training data by adding slightly modified copies of already existing data or newly created synthetic data from existing data.

decision trees

A machine learning algorithm that splits the data into branches at each level of decision-making. It allows for the visualization and interpretation of complex scenarios.

Deep Belief Network (DBN)

A generative graphical model, or alternatively a class of deep neural network, composed of multiple layers of latent variables ("hidden units").

deep learning

A subfield of machine learning that uses multi-layered artificial neural networks to deliver state-of-the-art accuracy in tasks such as object detection, speech recognition, and language translation.

Deep Q-Network (DQN)

An architecture that combines deep learning and reinforcement learning, particularly Q-Learning. It was used by DeepMind to play Atari games by only observing the pixels on the screen.

dimensionality reduction

The process of reducing the number of random variables under consideration, by obtaining a set of principal variables. It simplifies high-dimensional data while retaining its structure and usefulness.

embeddings

Embeddings are a type of representation learning that allows computers to understand the meaning of words or concepts by mapping them to points in a low-dimensional space. This makes it easier for machines to learn relationships between words and concepts, and to perform tasks such as text classification, natural language generation, and question answering.

ensemble models

Machine learning concept in which multiple models such as classifiers or experts are strategically generated and combined to solve a particular computational intelligence problem.

ethics in AI

The study of ethical issues emergent from or associated with the design, use, and implementation of AI. It ensures that AI systems are built and used in a way that aligns with human values and societal norms.

expert systems

A form of AI that attempts to reproduce the performance of a human expert in a specific field or area, typically through the application of rule-based algorithms and knowledge databases.

explainability in AI

The degree to which a machine learning model's predictions can be understood and interpreted by humans. It's an important factor in the trustworthiness of AI systems.

Extreme Gradient Boosting (XGBoost)

A scalable and accurate implementation of gradient boosting machines, built for model performance and computational speed.

Extreme Learning Machine (ELM)

A type of single-layer feedforward neural network with a single layer of hidden nodes.

fitting

Fitting is a process that is used to improve the accuracy of a machine learning model. It involves adjusting the parameters of the model until it makes predictions that are as close to the actual data as possible. The goal of fitting is to find a model that is both accurate and generalizable, meaning that it can make accurate predictions on new data that it has not seen before. See also **overfitting**.

Gated Recurrent Unit (GRU)

A type of recurrent neural network that is similar to LSTM but has a simpler structure.

Generative Adversarial Network (GAN)

A class of machine learning systems where two neural networks contest with each other in a game.

heuristic search

An approach in AI that uses techniques to speed up the process of solving a problem. It provides shortcuts in the search process by eliminating choices that are unlikely to lead to a solution.

Hidden Markov Model (HMM)

A statistical model where the system being modeled is assumed to be a Markov process with unobserved (hidden) states.

K-Nearest Neighbors (KNN)

A type of instance-based learning, or lazy learning, where the function is only approximated locally.

knowledge representation

A field within AI that focuses on representing information about the world in a form that a computer system can utilize to solve complex tasks such as diagnosing a medical condition or having a dialog in a natural language.

logic programming

A programming paradigm where program statements express facts and rules about problems within a system of formal logic.

Long Short-Term Memory (LSTM)

A type of recurrent neural network capable of learning order dependence in sequence prediction problems.

machine learning

A branch of AI that creates systems that learn and improve from experience without being explicitly programmed. It's focused on the development of programs that can access data and use it to learn and make predictions or decisions.

machine translation

A sub-field of computational linguistics that investigates the use of software to translate text or speech from one language to another.

Natural Language Generation (NLG)

The process of transforming structured data into natural language. It's used to create narratives and reports that people can understand from complex data sets.

Natural Language Processing (NLP)

A branch of AI that helps computers understand, interpret, and respond to human languages in a valuable way.

Natural Language Understanding (NLU)

A sub-category of NLP that focuses on machine reading comprehension. It deals with the complex and nuanced semantics of human language.

neural networks

A set of algorithms modeled after the human brain, designed to recognize patterns in complex data, and interpret sensory data through a kind of machine perception, labeling, or clustering raw input.

ontology

In the context of AI, it refers to a structured set of concepts or entities and their relationships that explain some domain of knowledge.

overfitting

A concept in machine learning where a statistical model fits the training data too closely. Overfitting occurs when the model is excessively complex, such as having too many parameters relative to the number of observations.

preprocessing

The preliminary data processing procedures that are applied to raw data to prepare it for machine learning. It includes data cleaning, transformation, normalization, and feature extraction.

Principal Component Analysis (PCA)

A technique used to emphasize variation and bring out strong patterns in a dataset.

Random Forests (RF)

A learning method that operates by constructing a multitude of decision trees at training time.

Recurrent Neural Network (RNN)

A class of artificial neural networks where connections between nodes form a directed graph along a temporal sequence.

regression

A supervised machine learning technique used to predict a continuous outcome. It tries to model the relationship between variables by fitting a curve to the observed data.

Reinforcement Learning (RL)

An area of machine learning where an agent learns to make decisions by performing actions and receiving rewards (or penalties) in a dynamic environment.

Reinforcement Learning with Human Feedback (RLHF)

A type of reinforcement learning that combines human feedback into the model training process.

robotics

A field intersecting AI and engineering, dedicated to the design, construction, and use of robots. AI-powered robots can perform tasks autonomously or semi-autonomously.

semi-supervised learning

A machine learning method that uses a combination of a small amount of labeled data and a large amount of unlabeled data for training. The goal is to use the unlabeled data to improve the learning accuracy.

simulation

The imitation of the operation of a real-world process or system over time. In AI, it's often used for training models, such as self-driving cars or game-playing bots, in a controlled and reproducible environment.

supervised learning

A type of machine learning where the model is trained on a labeled dataset. The model learns from past data inputs, then applies what it has learned to new data.

Support Vector Machine (SVM)

A type of supervised machine learning model used for classification and regression analysis.

transfer learning

A research problem in machine learning that focuses on storing knowledge gained while solving one problem and applying it to a different but related problem.

unsupervised learning

A type of machine learning where the model isn't given the correct answers. Instead, it finds structure in its input by itself, typically through clustering or through dimensionality reduction techniques.

EDUCATIONAL
PUBLISHING TERMS

adaptive learning technology
A technology that uses AI algorithms to adjust the path and pace of learning, tailored to the learner's needs.

assessment
A broad term in education that refers to the wide variety of methods or tools that educators use to evaluate, measure, and document the academic readiness, learning progress, skill acquisition, or educational needs of students.

backward design
A method of designing educational curriculum by setting goals before choosing instructional methods and forms of assessment. The philosophy is to 'begin with the end in mind.'

Bloom's Taxonomy
A classification system used by educators to create learning outcomes and assessments that are tied to higher-level cognitive skills. It is often used in the creation of textbooks and other educational materials.

Common Core State Standards (CCSS)
A set of high-quality academic standards in mathematics and English language arts/literacy (ELA). These learning goals outline what a student should know and be able to do at the end of each grade level.

Competency-Based Learning (or Competency-Based Education, CBE)
An educational approach that focuses on the student's demonstration of desired learning outcomes as central to the learning process. It is often characterized by flexible pacing and a mastery-based approach.

content correlation
The alignment of learning materials with educational standards and frameworks.

Criterion-Referenced Test (CRT)
An assessment that measures student performance against a fixed set of predetermined criteria or learning standards.

Diagnostic Assessment
An assessment method used to evaluate a student's knowledge, skills, and understandings before the instruction begins, and to reveal preconceptions or misconceptions that may affect how they interpret the instruction.

differentiated instruction
This is a teaching method where instruction is tailored to meet the diverse learning needs of students. In educational publishing, materials may be designed in a way that facilitates differentiated instruction.

Early Childhood Education (ECE)
A branch of education theory that relates to the teaching of young children (formally and informally) from birth up to the age of eight.

formative assessment
This refers to the evaluation of student comprehension and learning progression during the instructional process, often shaping upcoming instruction. Educational publishers may provide resources or materials designed to facilitate formative assessments.

high-stakes testing
This refers to tests with significant implications for the test taker, such as high school graduation exams, college entrance exams, and standardized state-level assessments.

Informal Assessment
Assessments that can be casual, unplanned, and occur in the daily classroom environment. These include observational assessments, anecdotal records, checklists, and rating scales.

instructional design

The practice of creating educational experiences or learning materials in a systematic and efficient manner to facilitate learning.

Item Response Theory (IRT)

A family of theories related to the design, analysis, and scoring of educational and psychological tests, questionnaires, and similar instruments where the aim is to discern and measure the level of a latent trait or interest in the subject.

Learning Management System (LMS)

A software application for the administration, documentation, tracking, reporting, automation, and delivery of educational courses, training programs, or learning and development programs.

learning objective

An explicit statement that describes what the learner will be able to do upon completion of a unit, course, lesson, or activity.

learning progression

Descriptions of the successively more sophisticated ways of thinking about a topic that can follow one another as children learn about and investigate a topic over a broad span of time.

learning styles

This term refers to the belief that individuals have different approaches to learning, and these preferences impact their academic performance. Materials may be designed to cater to different learning styles, like visual, auditory, reading/writing, and kinesthetic.

Norm-Referenced Test (NRT)

A type of test, assessment, or evaluation which yields an estimate of the position of the tested individual in a predefined population.

Pedagogical Content Knowledge (PCK)

This term refers to the blend of content knowledge and pedagogy that is specific to teaching. It's the kind of knowledge teachers need to take content understood at an advanced level and make it accessible to their students.

performance assessment

An assessment that requires students to perform tasks or activities that demonstrate their knowledge or skills. It goes beyond multiple-choice or fill-in-the-blank types of tests to allow the student to show what they can do.

prerequisite knowledge

The foundational information or skills that a learner must have prior to learning a new concept or skill.

Professional Development (PD)

Learning to earn or maintain professional credentials such as academic degrees to formal coursework, attending conferences, and informal learning opportunities situated in practice.

Response to Intervention (RTI)

A multi-tier approach to the early identification and support of students with learning and behavior needs.

rubric

A scoring tool used to interpret and grade students' work against criteria and standards.

scaffolding

This refers to the process of providing step-by-step support to enhance learning and aid in the mastery of tasks. It's often considered when creating educational resources.

scope and sequence

This term refers to the order in which educational material should be taught, starting from the basic concepts and moving to the more complex ones. It also outlines the objectives and skills that are to be achieved by the end of a certain time period.

summative assessment
This refers to the evaluation of student learning at the end of an instructional unit by comparing it against some standard or benchmark.

Universal Design for Learning (UDL)
A framework to improve and optimize teaching and learning for all people based on scientific insights into how humans learn.

PROOFREADING
CHARTS

Proofreading Charts

Spacing

SYMBOL	MEANING	MARKED EXAMPLE	FINAL SENTENCE
#	Add space	Roll on the#ground	Roll on the ground
⌢⌣	Close-up Space; Delete Space	Mal dives	Maldives
ℓ⌢⌣	Delete and Close up Space	You are mis-taken	You are mistaken
eq #	Equal Space Between Words	Kolkata| is| the| hub	Kolkata is the hub
□]	Indent 1-em space	□]Kolkata is the cultural capital	Kolkata is the cultural capital
⫿]	Indent 2-em spaces	tradition. ⫿]Yuba City is the	tradition. Yuba City is the
□	Insert 1-em space	includes:^sandwiches	includes: sandwiches
[2]	Insert 2-em spaces	includes:^sandwiches	includes: sandwiches
[3]	Insert 3-em spaces	who saw you?^The police	who saw you? The police
⧄	Insert 1-en space	How are you?^Fine	How are you? Fine
hr#	Insert hair space	Georg^ia	Georgia
|⌢⌣	Less Space	Roll on the|⌢⌣ ground	Roll on the ground
eq #	Make leading space equal between lines	>New York is >Hampshire was Towns denote	New York is Hampshire was Towns denote
loose	Too much space between words	This town is small (loose)	This town is small
tight	Too little space between words	This town is small (tight)	This town is small

Deletion and Insertion

SYMBOL	MEANING	MARKED EXAMPLE	FINAL SENTENCE
ꝯs	Insert and connect with character to the left	swing͜high	swings high
sꝯ	Insert and connect with character to the right	swing͜lowly	swing slowly
ꝯoꝯ	Insert letter	New Y͜rk	New York
is	Left out; insert	New York͜the	New York is the
ꝯeꝯ	Replace letter	N͜aw York	New York
⎰	Take out; delete	New York͜s	New York
⎽ℓ	Take out; delete	in ~~Hartford~~ Connecticut	in Connecticut

Punctuation and Math

SYMBOL	MEANING	MARKED EXAMPLE	FINAL SENTENCE
(mult sign)	Change to multiplication sign	5⊗5	5 × 5
(minus sign)	Change to minus sign	5 - 5	5 – 5
⌄	Insert apostrophe	New York͜s roads	New York's roads
[|]	Insert brackets	New York͜New York͜is	New York [New York] is
: |	Insert colon	as one follows͜one plan	as one follows: one plan
⌄,	Insert comma	New York͜New York	New York, New York

Proofreading Charts

SYMBOL	MEANING	MARKED EXAMPLE	FINAL SENTENCE
$\frac{1}{m}$	Insert em dash	On the way as we	On the way — as we
$\frac{1}{n}$	Insert en dash	130-147	130–147
(equals)	Insert equal sign	5 × 5 25	5 × 5 = 25
(set) !	Insert exclamation point	See you soon	See you soon!
/= /	Insert hyphen	pasteup	paste-up
∉/∌	Insert parenthesis	New York New York is	New York (New York) is
⊙	Insert period	New York It is	New York. It is
(set) ?	Insert question mark	Are you in New York.	Are you in New York?
ᵛ ᵛ	Insert quotation marks	The controversial topic	The "controversial" topic
⌃⁝	Insert semicolon	In New York we can	In New York; we can
(set) ≠	Insert slash	My pronouns are she her	My pronouns are she/her
ⱽ	Insert superscript	xn2	x^{n2}
ⱽ	Insert superscript with subscript	x xn2	$x^{n}{}_{2}$

Font Changes as Corrections

SYMBOL	MEANING	MARKED EXAMPLE	FINAL SENTENCE
c/sc	Capitals and small capitals	New York is	NEW YORK is
cap	Capital letter	new York	New York
l c	Lowercase letter	New York /s	New York is
l c	Lowercase word	New York is|THE hub	New York is the hub
bf	Set in boldface type	New York is the hub	New York is the **hub**
caps	Set in capitals	new york is the	NEW YORK IS THE
capitals	Set in capital italics	new york is	*NEW YORK IS*
ital	Set in italics	New York is	*New York* is
rom	Set in roman type	New York is the hub	New York is the hub
sm caps	Small capitals	New York is	NEW YORK is
wf	Wrong font	New York	New York

Proofreading Charts

Moving Type

SYMBOL	MEANING	MARKED EXAMPLE	FINAL SENTENCE
‖	Align type; no indent	The city of New York	The City of New York
(ctr)	Center	The northeastern city:]New York[	The Northeastern city: New York
(ctr)	Center vertically	New York { 42 in. 31 in. 40 in.	New York { 42 in. 31 in. 40 in.
⊔	Lower type or element	New York is	New York is
⊓	Raise type or element	New York is	New York is
(f.l.)	Flush left	The city [of New York	The city of New York
(fl.r.)	Flush right	The city] of New York	The city of New York
⊏	Move left	New York is	New York is
⊐	Move right	New York is	New York is
(no ¶)	No paragraph; run in	commerce. New York	commerce. New York
(RB)	Rebreak line	It is a northeastern city. It is very large.	It is a northeastern city. It is very large.
(run back)	Run back onto previous line	commerce in New York	commerce in New York
(RB fl.l.)	Start new line (but not new paragraph)	It is a northeastern city. It is very large.	It is a northeastern city. It is very large.
(¶)	Start new paragraph	commerce. New York	commerce. New York

63

Miscellaneous

SYMBOL	MEANING	MARKED EXAMPLE	FINAL SENTENCE
dropped copy	Insert matter omitted; refer to copy	New York east coast. *dropped copy*	New York is the hub of the east coast.
stet	Let it stand	New York is	New York is
4 1 3 2	Rearrange in order of numbers	4 1 2 5 3 the New York hub is	New York is the hub
spell out	Spell out	Use 5 oz.	Use five ounces
∿	Transpose	is New york the	New York is the

STANDARD
REFERENCES

STANDARD REFERENCES

The major reference works used in the publishing industry vary, depending on the type of work produced. These are the four primary references commonly used, but there are several additional works listed here that serve as references in the MS in Publishing program.

Associated Press Stylebook, **56th edition**

According to the publisher, "The 56th edition of *The Associated Press Stylebook and Briefing on Media Law* includes more than 300 new or revised entries, with chapters covering data journalism, business, religion, and sports terms, as well as media law, news values, punctuation, social media and polls and surveys, plus a new chapter on inclusive storytelling. This is the most referenced style guide in journalism." ISBN: 978-0-917360-70-1.

Publication Manual of the American Psychological Association, **Seventh Edition,** *2020*

The APA style manual website states that the manual is "the choice for writers, researchers, editors, students, and educators in the social and behavioral sciences, natural sciences, nursing, communications, education, business, engineering, and other fields."

Three editions:
Spiral 978-1-4338-3217-8
Paperback ISBN: 978-1433832161
Hardcover 978-1-4338-3215-4

The Chicago Manual of Style: The Essential Guide for Writers, Editors, and Publishers, **17th edition (University of Chicago Press)**

The preferred style guide for most trade book publishers, their website states that, "For more than one hundred years *CMS* has remained the definitive guide for anyone who works with words." It is considered "An indispensable reference for writers, editors, proofreaders, indexers, copywriters, designers, and publishers, informing the editorial canon with sound, definitive advice." ISBN: 978-0226287058

MLA Handbook, 9th edition **(Modern Languages Association)**

The MLA website calls their guide, "The comprehensive, go-to resource for writers of research papers, and anyone citing sources, from business writers, technical writers, and freelance writers and editors to student writers and the teachers and librarians collaborating with them. Intended for a variety of classroom contexts—middle school,

high school, and college courses in composition, communication, literature, language arts, film, media studies, digital humanities, and related fields."
ISBN: 978-1603293518

The Elements of Style, 4th edition
William Strunk and E.B. White
Originally published in 1918, this short book has taught the basics of English grammar to generations of writers. Author Stephen King believes that "...every aspiring writer should read *The Elements of Style*." There are many editions of the book, including an illustrated version by Maira Kalman in 2007, a version by Richard De A'Morelli, that adds two additional chapters, and an annotated version of the book published in 2020 (Tim Robert, editor).
ISBN: 9780205309023 (pb)

Dreyer's English: An Utterly Correct Guide to Clarity and Style
Benjamin Dreyer
Written by the longtime copy chief at Random House, the book was a *New York Times* bestseller. The *New York Times* review called it "A sharp, funny grammar guide they'll actually want to read."
ISBN: 978-0812985719 (pb)

EDItEUR ONIX Codelists
A comprehensive list of ONIX metadata codes and meanings, used in book metadata.
https://www.editeur.org/14/Code-Lists/#CodeLists

PUBLISHING
INDUSTRY
ORGANIZATIONS

PUBLISHING INDUSTRY ORGANIZATIONS

Descriptions of each organization are taken directly from their web site. This is by no means a comprehensive list. We have tried to include all the major industry organizations that serve publishers, writers, and industry partners.

American Booksellers Association

A national not-for-profit trade organization that supports the success of independent bookstores.
https://www.bookweb.org/

American Library Association

This organization provides leadership for the development, promotion, and improvement of library and information services and the profession of librarianship in order to enhance learning and ensure access to information for all.
https://www.ala.org/

American Society for Indexing (ASI)

The American Society for Indexing, Inc. (ASI) is a national association founded in 1968 to promote excellence in indexing and increase awareness of the value of well-written and well-designed indexes. A nonprofit educational and charitable organization, ASI serves indexers, librarians, abstractors, editors, publishers, database producers, data searchers, product developers, technical writers, academic professionals, researchers and readers, and others concerned with indexing. It is the only professional organization in the United States devoted solely to the advancement of indexing, abstracting and database construction. ASI encourages the participation of all persons, groups, and organizations interested in indexing and related methods of information retrieval.
https://www.asindexing.org

American Society of Magazine Editors (ASME)

An organization for the editorial leaders of magazines and websites published in the United States. ASME "strives to defend the First Amendment, support the development of journalism and promote the editorial integrity of print and digital publications. ASME sponsors the National Magazine Awards in association with the Columbia Journalism School, conducts training programs for reporters and editors and publishes the ASME Guidelines for Editors and Publishers (https://www.asme.media/editorial-guidelines).
https://www.asme.media/

Association of American Literary Agents

An organization of professionals working at literary agencies, dedicated to helping their members develop and maintain their professional skills through education, networking, mentorship, and a commitment to the highest ethical standards.
https://aalitagents.org/

Association of American Publishers

The AAP represents the leading book, journal, and education publishers in the United States on matters of law and policy, advocating for outcomes that incentivize the publication of creative expression, professional content, and learning solutions.
https://publishers.org/

Association of Catholic Publishers

A collegial and collaborative organization composed of Catholic publishers and producers of Catholic content across various media including books, audio, video, and music regardless of format (e.g., digital vs. print). The ACP supports a viable, vibrant, and diverse Catholic publishing environment throughout North America and beyond. It seeks to provide visibility to, advocacy for, and sustainability of published Catholic content.
https://www.catholicpublishers.org/

Association of Magazine Media (MPA)

See **News/Media Alliance**

Association of Publishers for Special Sales

APSS is a nonprofit trade association of authors and independent publishers with the mission of building successful writing and publishing businesses.
https://pro.bookapss.org/

Association of University Presses

The Association of University Presses advances the essential role of a global community of publishers whose mission is to ensure academic excellence and cultivate knowledge.
https://aupresses.org/

Audio Publishers Association

Formed in 1986, the Audio Publishers Association (APA) is a not-for-profit trade association that advocates the common, collective business interests of audio publishers. The APA consists of audio publishing

companies and suppliers, distributors, and retailers of spoken word products and allied fields related to the production, distribution, and sale of audiobooks.
https://www.audiopub.org/

BookScan

This company tracks about 85% of trade book sales sold through the major retailers, independent bookstores, and others. A major source of information for publishers, agent, and authors, BookScan provides comprehensive sales tracking for digital and physical book sales.

Book Industry Communication (BIC)

UK organization that supports the book industry supply chain. They offer leadership through listening and building best practice in the book supply chain to sustain the health of the publishing industry. From Thema codes to metadata, sustainability to ONIX, their expert-led hub provides all the resources needed.
https://bic.org.uk/

Book Industry Study Group (BISG)

A membership organization comprised of a diverse slate of publishers, manufacturers, wholesalers and distributors, libraries, retailers and industry partners, organized by committees dedicated to solving problems that affect two or more parts of the industry, with five core practice areas: metadata, rights, supply chain, subject codes (BISAC), and workflow.
https://www.bisg.org/

Book Manufacturers' Institute

BMI supports book manufacturing leaders in their work to drive the promotion, efficiency, and growth of book markets for readers and educators in North America. BMI member companies range from full-service book manufacturers to those specializing in the digital print market, specialty binderies, component printers, packagers, equipment manufacturers, and suppliers of a variety of materials and services.
https://www.bmibook.com/

Children's Book Council

The CBC is a nonprofit trade association of children's book publishers in North America, dedicated to supporting the industry and promoting children's books and reading.
https://www.cbcbooks.org/

Edelweiss

A digital catalog platform that helps publishers manage their front-list catalogs and review copies as well as their sales and marketing processes. The platform is host to 95% of all US frontlist for the major US publishers.

EDItEUR

An international standards organization with over 110 members from 25 countries, including North America (Canada, United States), most European countries, and the Asia-Pacific region (Australia, China, Japan, Korea). EDItEUR has developed a number of key standards that are already internationally used within the books and serials supply chains to facilitate e-commerce, enable the transmission of rich metadata records, and use existing identifiers.
https://www.editeur.org/

Editorial Freelancers Association

According to the EFA web site, their organization "advances excellence among our dynamic community of freelance editorial professionals by providing opportunities for business development, learning, and networking. Our resources help our members and their clients build successful collaborations."
https://www.the-efa.org/

Evangelical Christian Publishing Association

ECPA is the association of Christian publishers, who work together to strengthen and lead the industry through connection, education, and resources.
https://www.ecpa.org/

Graphic Artists' Guild

The Graphic Artists Guild's primary purpose is to help their members compete effectively in an ever-changing field, enabling graphic artists and other design professionals to build and maintain successful careers by providing them with skills and support—from advice on the daily tasks of running a creative business. Guild members are creative professionals and those studying to become creative professionals.
https://graphicartistsguild.org/

Independent Book Publishers Association

The IBPA is a not-for-profit membership organization serving and leading the independent publishing community through advocacy, education, and tools for success. With over 4,100 members, IBPA is

the largest publishing trade association in the U.S.
https://www.ibpa-online.org/

Independent Publishers Caucus (IPC)

Formed to foster a sense of community among companies helping to keep the written word alive. Now more than ever, independent media is crucial to keeping discussion moving in the public square. IPC understands that for the independent publishing world to thrive, it's important to share information about what works and what doesn't, getting the attention of booksellers and the media, and understanding the financial realities that come with running a publishing company on a day-to-day basis.
https://www.indiepubs.org

Independent Publishers Guild

IPG is an independent distributor of books, ebooks, and audiobooks from publishers around the world, and a top 10 supplier of book content to Amazon, Barnes & Noble, independent bookstores, libraries, and specialty markets, in addition to thousands of retailers globally.
https://www.ipgbook.com/

International Association of Museum Publishers

The International Association of Museum Publishers (IAMP) provides a forum for museum publishers worldwide to exchange ideas and discuss matters of importance in the field.
https://museumpublishers.wordpress.com/

International Board on Books for Young People

Founded in Zurich in 1953, IBBY is a non-profit organization which represents an international network of people from all over the world who are committed to bringing books and children together. Their mission includes promoting international understanding through children's books; giving children everywhere the opportunity to have access to books with high literary and artistic standards; encouraging the publication and distribution of quality children's books, especially in developing countries; providing support and training for those involved with children and children's literature; stimulate research and scholarly works in the field of children's literature; protecting and upholding the Rights of the Child according to the UN Convention on the Rights of the Child.
https://www.ibby.org/

International Literacy Association

The ILA, formerly the International Reading Association, is a professional membership organization of more than 300,000 literacy educators, researchers, and experts across 128 countries. Through their work, they support literacy professionals and educators from every corner of the world and advocate for children's rights to read and to excellent literacy instruction in reading, writing, communicating, and critical thinking.
https://www.literacyworldwide.org/

Mystery Writers of America (MWA)

MWA is dedicated to promoting higher regard for crime writing and recognition and respect for those who write within the genre. They provide scholarships for writers, sponsor MWA Literacy programs, sponsor symposia and conferences, present the Edgar Awards, and conduct other activities to further a better appreciation and higher regard for crime writing.
https://mysterywriters.org/

National Association of Science Writers

Established in 1934, NASW is a community of journalists, authors, editors, producers, public information officers, students and people who write and produce material intended to inform the public about science, health, engineering, and technology. NASW promotes the professional interests of science writers nationally and globally, plays an active role in supporting efforts to ensure writers are paid for their work, and advocates for copyright protections for writers.
https://www.nasw.org/

National Book Critics Circle

Founded in 1974, the NBCC honors outstanding writing and fosters a national conversation about reading, criticism, and literature. Serving about 800 members, the NBCC includes critics, authors, literary bloggers, book publishing professionals, student members, and friends. Membership is open to freelance and staff book reviewers, associate nonvoting members, student members, and friends. Full members receive access to tips on book reviewing, an annually updated guide to publications that accept freelance pitches for reviews, the ability to nominate titles for their annual awards and elect board members, plus a variety of discounts on literary magazines.
https://www.bookcritics.org/

National Book Foundation

The mission of the NBF is to celebrate the best literature published in the United States, expand its audience, and ensure that books have a prominent place in our culture. They present the National Book Awards every year.
https://www.nationalbook.org/

National Council of Teachers of English

NCTE supports teachers and their students in classrooms, on college campuses, and in online learning environments.

For more than 100 years, NCTE has worked with its members to offer journals, publications, and resources; to further the voice and expertise of educators as advocates for their students at the local and federal levels; and to share lesson ideas, research, and teaching strategies through its Annual Convention and other professional learning events.
https://ncte.org/

New York Book Forum

Dedicated to building bridges between the entire book publishing world and the public with an emphasis on the importance of reading and promoting literacy.
newyorkbookforum.org.

News/Media Alliance

The voice of the news and magazine industries, the News/Media Alliance is a nonprofit organization headquartered in the Washington, D.C. area that represents nearly 2,000 diverse publishers in the United States— from digital-only and digital-first to print.

The organization has grown through the combining of a range of news and media publishing associations, most recently including a merger with The Association of Magazine Media (MPA) in 2022.
https://www.newsmediaalliance.org/

PEN America

Founded in 1922, PEN America stands at the intersection of literature and human rights to protect free expression in the United States and worldwide. They champion the freedom to write, recognizing the power of the word to transform the world. Their mission is to unite writers and their allies to celebrate creative expression and defend the liberties that make it possible.
https://pen.org/

Poetry Society of America

The nation's oldest poetry organization, the Poetry Society of America was founded in 1910. Its mission is to build a larger and more diverse audience for poetry, to encourage a deeper appreciation of the vitality and breadth of poetry in the cultural conversation, to support poets through an array of programs and awards, and to place poetry at the crossroads of American life.
https://poetrysociety.org/

Poets and Writers

Founded in 1970, Poets and Writers is the nation's largest nonprofit organization serving creative writers and foster their professional development, to promote communication throughout the literary community, and to help create an environment in which literature can be appreciated by the widest possible public.
https://www.pw.org/

Print and Graphic Communications Association

In 2023, the Printing Industries Alliance and the Graphic Arts Association consolidated to form one of the nation's largest regional trade associations for the printing industry. The Association provides business support services and connections to the paper, print, packaging, and mailing community in New York State, New Jersey, Pennsylvania, and Delaware.
https://printcommunications.org/

Protestant Church-Owned Publishers Association

An international association of non-profit, Protestant denominational publishers and other non-profit Christian publishers who serve one or more Protestant denominations through the content they create, publish, or distribute. Their publishing company members publish content using a wide range of print and digital media and serve Christians through congregations, higher education, outdoor ministries, libraries, and other organizations.
https://www.pcpaonline.org/

Publishers Advertising and Marketing Association

Founded in 1921, PAMA offers professionals the opportunity to meet some of publishing's most prominent leaders, network, and share innovative marketing ideas with peers, and gain insights into the book industry.
https://pama-ny.org/

The Publishers Association of the West

PubWest is a national trade organization of publishers and of associated publishing-related members. The organization is dedicated to offering professional education, providing publishing-related benefits, creating opportunities for our members and associate members to do business, speaking as an advocate for members, recognizing outstanding achievement in publishing, and providing a forum for networking to our publishing and associate members from across the United States and Canada.
https://pubwest.org/

Publishers Publicity Association (PPA)

The Publishers' Publicity Association is a non-profit, professional group open to publicists of book publishing houses, as well as public relations personnel in related media. Its purpose is to raise the professional level of book publishers' publicity by conducting research into all media and by providing a meeting place for the discussion and exchange of ideas and techniques.
https://publisherspublicityassociation.square.site/

Romance Writers of America

RWA is a nonprofit trade association whose mission is to advance the professional and common business interests of career-focused romance writers through networking and advocacy and by increasing public awareness of the romance genre.
https://www.rwa.org/

Science Fiction and Fantasy Writers of America

Founded in 1965, SFWA is an organization for published authors and industry professionals in the fields of science fiction, fantasy, and related genres. Membership is open to authors, artists, and other industry professionals, including graphic novelists.
https://www.sfwa.org/

Society for Scholarly Publishing

Founded in 1978, the SSP is a nonprofit organization formed to promote and advance communication among all sectors of the scholarly publication community through networking, information dissemination, and facilitation of new developments in the field.
https://www.sspnet.org/

Society of Children's Book Writers and Illustrators

SCBWI is a global community of writers, illustrators, translators, publishers, librarians, advocates, and other industry professionals working to establish a more imaginative and inclusive world through the power of children's literature. Their mission is to support the creation of an abundance of quality children's books, so that young people everywhere have the books they need and deserve.
https://www.scbwi.org/

Society of Illustrators

Founded in 1901, the mission of the Society of Illustrators is to promote the art of illustration, to appreciate its history and evolving nature through exhibitions, lectures and education, and to contribute the service of its members to the welfare of the community at large.
https://societyillustrators.org/

Women's Media Group

WMG is a New York City-based nonprofit association of women who have achieved prominence in the many fields of media—print and digital book, magazine, and newspaper publishing; film and television; and online and other digital media. Members meet to collaborate with, learn from, inform, and support one another. The organization is also dedicated to mentoring young women interested in pursuing media careers.
https://www.womensmediagroup.org/

Writers Guild of America

The WGA is the joint efforts of two different American labor unions, The Writers Guild of America, East, headquartered in NYC and The Writers Guild of America, West, headquartered in Los Angeles, representing writers in film, television, radio, and online media. Although each organization operates independently, they perform some common activities, including negotiating contracts and launching strike actions in unison.
https://www.wga.org/

Young Adult Library Services Association

A division of the American Library Association, YALSA brings together key stakeholders from the areas of libraries, education, research, out of school time, youth development, and more to develop and deliver resources to libraries that expand their capacity to support teen learning and enrichment and to foster healthy communities.
https://www.ala.org/yalsa/

APPENDICES

Appendices

Elements of a Marketing Kit
- Press Release
- Contact Information/Business card
- Sell Sheet (includes: title, author, book description, ISBN, binding, trim size, number of pages, price, order information)
- Author bio and photo
- Book jacket or cover
- Reviews and/or endorsements
- Sample chapter or review copy
- Overview of Marketing efforts

APPENDIX B
Elements of a Press or Media Kit
- Press Release
- Contact information
- Book cover
- Book sample
- Author bio and photo
- Author Q&A
- Testimonials/Reviews
- Imagery as appropriate (author photo or book cover)
- Tour information if available

APPENDIX C
Elements of a Press Release
- Contact information
- A compelling headline
- Brief blurb/s about the book
- One to three paragraphs describing the book
- Book cover (optional but preferred)
- Brief author bio (including any weblinks)
- Author photo (with photographer credit)
- Company boilerplate and credit lines
- Author's social media information

APPENDIX D

Front Matter

The first section of a book, front matter, includes all the preliminary text for the book. The list below reflects the usual sequence of each element, but not every element is included. Typically, most titles will only have the half title, title page, copyright page, and contents page.

Front matter includes:

Acknowledgements

Card page

Copyright page (can include copyright notice, publisher's name and address, date of publication, number of printings, ISBN, CIP data, any disclaimers or warranties)

Contents page

Dedication

Foreword

Half title page

Introduction

Preface

Prologue

Reviews

Title page

Back Matter

The supplementary pages at the end of a book. The list below reflects the usual sequence of each element, but every element isn't necessarily included. Most fiction titles will have a back of book ad or an author bio, while nonfiction back matter tends to be more robust with an index and/or bibliography.

Back matter includes:

Afterword

Appendix

Artwork and photography credits

Author bio

Author note

Back of book ad

Bibliography

Colophon

Contributor list or bios

Epilogue

Glossary

Index

Suggested reading

CONTRIBUTOR
BIOS

Contributor Bios

Ken Brooks

President, Treadwell Media Group

Professor Brooks is president of Treadwell Media Group, a product development, supply chain, and strategy consulting firm focused on the education and trade publishing sectors.

Previously, he was the Chief Content Officer for the Academic and Professional Learning division of Wiley, where his responsibilities included development and production of higher education, reference, test prep, and trade titles in print and digital formats. Over the course of his career, Brooks has founded digital services companies both in the US and abroad; a public domain publishing imprint; and a distribution-center based print-on-demand operation and has worked in trade, professional, higher education, and K-12 publishing sectors.

Brooks holds Bachelor's and Master's degrees in industrial engineering and a Master's Degree in computer science from Georgia Tech, where he also mentors graduate students in Educational Technology.

Joseph Caserto

Joseph Caserto Art Direction + Design

Professor Caserto is an award-winning graphic artist, educator, and consultant, who is based in the Hudson Valley and New York City, specializing in publication art direction and design. Caserto earned a BFA with honors in Graphic Design from Pratt Institute, where he completed one of the first classes that covered the Mac as a design tool. With over 30 years of professional experience, he is currently a freelance art director and designer whose clients have included *Billboard, BusinessWeek, Fortune, Marie Claire*, and *Vibe* magazines. He has won American Graphic Design Awards from GD USA magazine annually, since 2008, when he also received a Create Award. He is a member of Freelancers Union and has been a member of AIGA, Graphic Artists Guild, and the Society of Publication Designers (SPD).

Britney Fitzgerald

Assistant Director of Communications, American Museum of Natural History

Professor Fitzgerald is a Pace Publishing alum who has worked in New York's editorial and social media sectors for over a decade. Her writing has been featured in The Huffington Post, Parents magazine, Brit+Co, The Knot, and more. She has managed social strategy at several magazines and for an advertising agency. She is the head of social media at the American Museum of Natural History. Fitzgerald lives in Brooklyn with her husband and a French bulldog, Sir Walter.

Vincent Forgione
Operations Manager, Hearst Business Communications/FCW Division

Professor Forgione has more than 20 years of experience in media and communication. He graduated from Ithaca College with a Bachelor's degree in Television/Radio and earned a Master's degree in Public and Organizational Relations from Montclair State University. He has worked on the launch of NewsTalk Television, a cable television network that was a predecessor to FoxNews and MSNBC, managed public relations video projects for Edelman Public Relations, and spent over 16 years at Condé Nast leading production teams on various magazine brands such as *The New Yorker* and *Wired*. He currently leads production and operations on a B2B brand at Hearst Corporation while teaching courses in media and communication.

David Hetherington
Vice President, Global Business Development, Books International Inc.

Professor Hetherington's publishing portfolio reflects a broad range of responsibilities including both VP of Manufacturing as well as VP of Financial Planning for Simon & Schuster's Higher Education Group. In addition, Hetherington has held other senior leadership roles in Finance, Operations, and Sales at *Reader's Digest*, Wolters Kluwer Health, Columbia University Press, and Baker & Taylor. He also served in senior roles in the book publishing software industry including COO of Klopotek North America and as CMO of knk Software LP.

He holds a Bachelor's degree in business administration from Thomas Edison University and an MBA in Corporate Finance from Fairleigh Dickinson University. He also sits on the boards of the Book Industry Study Group and the Book Manufacturers Institute.

Eileen Kreit
Full-time Faculty, MS in Publishing

Professor Kreit is a lifelong reader and book lover. She spent 32 years at Penguin Random House, joining the Putnam Berkley Publishing Group as Sales Assistant after graduating from the University of Massachusetts. After 15 years in sales leadership and management, Kreit moved to the editorial side as Vice President and Publisher of Puffin Books. Rising to President in 2007, she worked with authors including S.E. Hinton, Judy Blume, Mildred D. Taylor, Laurie Halse Anderson, Sarah Dessen, the collective works of Roald Dahl, and the Puffin Classics publishing program. In 2018, she transitioned to Vice President, Business Development, Viking Children's Books and Philomel Books, where she expanded classic brands and created new publishing for legacy characters of the publishing industry including Corduroy, Madeline, Pippi Longstocking, Encyclopedia Brown, and many others.

Paul Levitz
Former President, DC Comics

Professor Levitz is a comic fan (*The Comic Reader*), editor (Batman, among many titles), writer (*Legion of Super-Heroes*, including four NY Times Best Sellers), executive (30 years at DC, ending as President and Publisher), historian (*75 Years of DC Comics: The Art of Modern Myth-Making*, published by Taschen), and educator (including teaching a course on "The American Graphic Novel" at Columbia and Princeton, as well as "Transmedia and The Future of Publishing" in Pace's M.S. in Publishing Program, and graphic novel related courses on the undergraduate level). He won two consecutive annual Comic Art Fan Awards for Best Fanzine, received Comic-con International's Inkpot Award, the prestigious Bob Clampett Humanitarian Award, and the Comics Industry Appreciation Award from ComicsPro. His Taschen book won the Eisner Award, the Eagle Award, and Munich's Peng Pris. His most recent book is *AVENGERS: WAR ACROSS TIME* with artist Alan Davis. Levitz was inducted into the Will Eisner Hall of Fame, comics' most prestigious honor. Levitz also serves on the board of the Clarion Foundation and Boom! Studios.

Nellie McKesson
Founder and CEO, Hederis

Professor McKesson has over a dozen years of experience in publishing. She spent the early years of her career doing hands-on book production and layout, and then moved into more technical and managerial roles. As the market for ebooks began to rise, she taught herself web development and was an early evangelist for using web technologies in the book production process.

Jessica C. Napp
Director of Publicity, Rizzoli New York

Professor Napp (Class of 2000) is the Director of Publicity for Rizzoli New York. One to the most respected illustrated book publishers in the world, Rizzoli specializes in fashion and luxury lifestyle brands, art-architecture-photography monographs, cookbooks, and pop culture tomes.

Sister company Rizzoli Bookstore is one of the most celebrated independent bookstores in the world, with locations in New York (NoMad) and Milan (The Galleria). She has worked on book PR campaigns for Kim Kardashian, Diane Keaton, Whoopi Goldberg, the Bob's Burgers franchise, the Macy's Thanksgiving Day Parade, plus countless others. Before joining Rizzoli she worked in publicity departments at Simon & Schuster, Little Brown, and Abrams/Stewart, Tabori & Chang. She lives in Hoboken, NJ, with her husband and two Shih Tzus.

Patricia Payton
Senior Manager, Provider Relations, ProQuest

Professor Payton is a metadata expert with knowledge of bibliographic standards, identifiers, and data analysis. As Senior Manager, Provider Relations, for ProQuest, part of Clarivate, she is responsible for communicating book and journal metadata requirements and best practices to publishers of all sizes.

Payton has over 20 years of experience in bookselling, library eBook platforms, and international book markets. She holds a Master's degree in Library Information Science specializing in Digital Libraries (Rutgers University) as well as an MBA (Kent State University).

In addition to serving as an Adjunct Lecturer for Pace University, she works within the Book Industry Study Group and the Book Industry Communications organization to help shape industry metadata practices. She lives in New Jersey and enjoys reading nonfiction works.

Jennifer Romanello
Associate Director, MS in Publishing

Professor Romanello began her career in book publishing as a publicity assistant at Macmillan and its imprints, Scribner and Atheneum. She then moved on to Dutton, where she eventually rose to Associate Director of Publicity and worked with a roster of critically acclaimed authors including Julia Alvarez, Joyce Carol Oates, and Jamaica Kincaid. In 1995 she joined Warner Books, now Grand Central Publishing, an imprint of Hachette. She was VP, Executive Director of Publicity there for many years and worked with a wide range of bestselling authors including Nicholas Sparks, David Baldacci, Nelson DeMille, and Brad Meltzer, among others.

She was most recently VP, Director of Publicity at Simon & Schuster Children's Publishing. Some of the authors she worked with at S&S include Cassandra Clare, Mike Lupica, Jennifer Weiner, Tomie dePaola, Alex Morgan, and Derek Jeter.

Contributor Bios

Romanello is currently Associate Director of the MS in Publishing Program at Pace University. She completed her MFA in Creative Writing with Distinction from Hofstra University and her poems have been published in *Italian-Americana, Paterson Literary Review, Red Fern Review, Ovunque Siamo*, and VIA: *Voices in Italiana-Americana*. Her poems "Omphalos" (2018) and "I terri" (2015) received first place in the Concorso Internationale di Poesia held in Messina, Sicily. She is working on a novel and poetry collection.

Kirsten Sandberg
Editor-in-Chief, Blockchain Research Institute

Professor Sandberg is a writer, editor, and consultant who works with executives and advisory boards to shape their publishing strategies in corporate and nonprofit settings. She is currently editor-in-chief of the Blockchain Research Institute and a member of the editorial advisory board of the *Journal of Business Models*. She has extensive experience in negotiating publishing agreements and turning knowledge and expertise into branded content for diverse audiences. For over a decade, she was an executive editor at the Harvard Business Review Press, where she specialized in strategy, technology, and finance. She started her media career as a computer graphics designer in the newsroom of WEEK-TV, an NBC affiliate at the time. Sandberg holds a B.A. in English and TV/Radio Production from Bradley University and began an M.A. in English at Marquette University. She is a Chicago Cubs fan by birth and a Yankees fan by naturalization.

Manuela Soares
Director, MS in Publishing

Prior to being named as Director in 2018, Soares had been a full-time faculty member in the MS in Publishing program since 2004. She has introduced several initiatives in the program, including One-to-One Mentoring every semester in addition to many other opportunities for networking and jobs.

Soares is also the Director of Pace University Press, overseeing the publication of journals and books, including the prestigious Woolf Studies Journal. Soares also works with Pace undergraduate and graduate faculty on creating text materials for programs, courses, and conferences.

In her over thirty-year career, Soares worked in both magazine and book publishing as a writer and editor, most recently as the Managing Editor at Scholastic, where she oversaw the publication of the Harry Potter series in addition to managing their hardcover imprints. Prior to that she was a Senior Editor at Rizzoli International, acquiring books in a variety of disciplines.

She is on the Editorial Board of *Publishing Research Quarterly*, where many of the program's thesis papers have been published in abbreviated form. Her own published work includes fiction and nonfiction..

Jason Wells

Marketing Director, APA Style, APA Books, LifeTools Nonfiction, and Magination Press, Children's Books, The American Psychological Association

Professor Wells is the Book Marketing Director at the American Psychological Association, where he and his team promote APA Books, APA Videos, APA Style, Life Tools, and Magination Press Children's Books. Previously he worked for almost 15 years at Abrams, where he invented and maintained for over a decade the marketing and publicity activities for the bestselling Diary of a Wimpy Kid series, among other bestselling and award-winning titles. Professor Wells has also held marketing and publicity roles at Simon & Schuster, Penguin Random House, Disney, and Rodale. He lives in Washington, DC, has previously taught at the Columbia Publishing Course, and has a master's degree in information science.

Veronica Wilson

National Digital Sales Director, Dotdash Meredith

Veronica serves as National Digital Sales Director for PeopleEnEspañol.com, at Dotdash Meredith, where she is responsible for driving advertising revenue. Prior to *People en Espanol* she worked at The Nielsen Company, as Business Development Director from 2017-2019. She was Associate Publisher–Sales at Meredith Corporation from 2009-2017, for Latino focused lifestyle and parenthood brands, Associate Publisher–Sales at Conde Nast for the Bridal Group in 2008, and Time Inc./Essence from 1999-2008, where she last held the position of National Ad Sales Director.

Professor Wilson holds a M.S. degree from Pace University and a B.B.A. degree from Temple University (Philadelphia, PA). She lives in Brooklyn, NY, and is an avid global traveler.

Words We Use was published
by Pace University Press

Cover and Interior Layouts by Sara Yager
The journal was typeset in Myraid Pro
and printed by Lightning Source in La Vergne, Tennessee

Pace University Press

Director: Manuela Soares
Faculty Advisor: Eileen Kreit
Production Consultant: Joseph Caserto
Production Associate: Lucely Garcia
Graduate Assistants: Erin Hurley and Kayleigh Woltal
Student Aide: Liz Abrams

www.ingramcontent.com/pod-product-compliance
Lightning Source LLC
Chambersburg PA
CBHW072207270326
41930CB00011B/2567